"Over a 40-year career in business, I read and was formed by some of the Masters: Drucker, Peters, Porter, Collins, Lencioni, et al. Never, however, have I read a book that better-integrated leadership principles, business imperatives, cultural observation, Christian spirituality, and missionary initiative. When you finish, you will not only be wiser about what it takes to run a successful enterprise; you'll find yourself challenged to become a better version of your best self."

Brian J. Gail
Former CEO and best-selling author of the *Fatherless* series

"Peter Darcy provides the insight and information needed by every priest and religious – this is the information not taught in seminary. How to run a non-profit organization by remaining focused on its mission and treating people with the respect they deserve. As Darcy emphasizes, 'leadership is not management,' and this book will teach its readers the vital difference."

Deal Hudson
Founder of *Crisis* magazine, *The Christian Review*, and author of *How to Keep from Losing Your Mind*

"This book is full of insight for those of us serving the mission of the church. Anyone in pastoral ministry will benefit from the no-nonsense look at basic issues of operations and leadership found in these pages. I loved reading it and plan to keep it handy as a companion for the mission."

Rev. James E. Molgano
Catholic diocesan priest and retired pastor

NO-NONSENSE
Non-Profit

Leadership Principles for
Church & Charity

PETER DARCY

Books and materials published by Strength of Soul Books may be purchased for mentoring, spiritual growth, evangelization, and promotional use. Please visit us at www.strengthofsoulbooks.com or contact us at publisher@strengthofsoulbooks.com.

This work is a revised and updated version of *Mister Buddy's Guide to Non-Profit Leadership: Principles for Success in a Charitable World* (Boiling Springs, PA: Tremendous Leadership, 2019).

First Edition

ISBN: 978-1-7332654-2-3

eBook ISBN: 978-1-7332654-3-0

For

*Rich Clair, Larry Jenkins, Frank Ruddy,
Fr. Lou Roberts, and Fr. Jerome Herman, all of
whom mentored me without even trying.*

Contents

Author's Prologue

A few years ago, after leaving a very satisfying and wonderful non-profit mission, I wrote a draft of this work as an aid to the leader who replaced me. It never got out of the rough draft stage, however, and I never sent it to him because it looked like he was performing very well without need of my advice. Frankly, I was delighted the organization was in such competent hands.

The draft sat in my computer for a couple of years, but it seemed to be begging to come to light after so long. Recently, I decided to dust it off and re-work it to apply to a wider segment of leaders in the non-profit world. I hope that the effort of putting these ideas down on paper will be of service to someone who aspires to be a leader in any noble mission that seeks to make the world a better place.

No-Nonsense Non-Profit: Leadership Principles for Church and Charity is full of advice-giving and tidbits ("what worked for me"), quaint personal anecdotes, a few inspirational stories, and my idea of best practices in the non-profit sector. Who doesn't need solid advice in the rough-and-tumble world of helping people? Why reinvent the wheel if someone else has already built a good one? It is, in all aspects, a non-nonsense manual on leading and running non-profits, as its title professes.

Even though this work was written from the background of non-profits that were not churches, the principles can be equally applied to the running of churches and parishes, which are non-profit, charitable organizations in the fullest sense of the word. Rather than re-write significant sections of the book to tailor them to clergy – who I hope will benefit greatly from this work – I chose to trust the intelligence of the reader to make a certain translation while reading. For example, passages that refer to a board of directors, legal authority, etc. can be easily thought of as one's "bishop", "religious superiors", "finance council", "oversight committee", or "vestry", as the case may be! A similar mental adaptation may be necessary in areas of scale (small vs. large organizations) or scope (local vs. national or international mission). The differing circumstances of each ministry are less critical factors because this book is about principles, not a directory for managing any particular organization.

The goal of *No-Nonsense Non-Profit* is to break down the business of running a charity or church to certain core principles in five areas: 1) leadership, 2) promotion, 3) mission, 4) organization, and 5) performance. There are eight principles in each of the five areas – as luck would have it, the biblical number forty – constituting a *tour de force* of short essays for the inquiring mind. (Short bursts of insight work best for busy people.) That last area, performance, is the stuff of an entire industry of motivational books these days, and you will find many good references for further reading in the "Helpful Resources" section at the back of the book.

I intend this book to be especially helpful to new leaders who haven't yet been exposed to the complexity of running a church or non-profit mission, but it can also serve as a refresher course for those who have been around the block in charitable work. If you have never worked in the non-profit field, the material in these pages will help you become an effective leader; if you're already an old pro, perhaps it will make you an even better leader and a better person.

Before jumping into the material, I should note that I use the "he" pronoun throughout the book because, contrary to many other languages, English has not yet figured out a way to speak of the two genders with a single pronoun. I am not a fan of the "singular *they*" either, which, in any case, has not become a standard way of writing except on social media. So, until literary civilization works out that little anomaly, it is easier to write from my side of the ledger to an audience that is largely male, knowing that female readers and leaders are capable of turning "he" into "she" whenever necessary.

Peter Darcy
Easter, 2020

When Leaders Are Absent

Like many good things in life, we only appreciate the blessings of leadership when we are deprived of them.

Most of us take leaders for granted because leadership is often a behind-the-scenes, thankless job, the details of which few people see. We mourn the loss of good leadership when it is *absent* because only its absence gives us a clue as to how much leaders do for us in silent ways while the rest of us cruise along on the surface of life enjoying the benefits of their hard work. If you ask yourself how important good leadership is to any human venture, you won't have to look far for an answer. Let's take just one famous example: the *Titanic*.

Virtually everyone in the Western world knows the story of the epic *Titanic* disaster in 1912. It was, of course, fundamentally a business venture for the British company, the White Star Line. It was not a charitable mission, but the leadership lessons we can derive from that tragedy are striking. Starting with the leadership failures surrounding the *Titanic* misadventure, let's begin with the most serious.

Leadership Failure #1 – dereliction of duty

Captain Edward J. Smith, an experienced British Royal Navy officer, drove the *Titanic* "full steam ahead" through an ocean full of icebergs with the ambition of setting a new trans-Atlantic passage record to New York. That act easily qualifies Captain Smith as the all-time winner of the "What Was He Thinking?" Award. Pressed for time, Captain Smith cancelled the customary lifeboat drill with passengers the day before the *Titanic* set sail. That same day, Smith dismissed an officer who took the key to the binocular case with him, thus depriving the *Titanic*'s crow's nest lookouts of their binoculars to scan for icebergs. Smith went to bed after a banquet held in his honor the night of the disaster, even though the ship was heading into very dangerous waters, and was awakened by the ship's collision with the iceberg. The Captain failed to maintain a dedicated line for wireless communication with other ships because his communications officer was too busy sending the first-class passengers' cables back to the mainland detailing the adventures of their pleasure cruise. Virtually nothing is known of Captain Smith's final two hours on the *Titanic*.

Leadership Failure #2 – negligent oversight

The year before the *Titanic* sailed, the same Captain Edward Smith was at the helm of the *Titanic*'s sister ship, the *Olympic*, which collided with a British warship, the RMS *Hawke,* near the Isle of Wight. A Navy investigation laid the blame for the incident squarely on Captain Smith. Knowing of this catastrophic event in Smith's recent history, the *Titanic*'s supervising authority, the White Star Fleet, nonetheless chose Smith to be captain of the *Titanic*. That esteemed committee deserves the "What *Were They* Thinking?" Award, which is given for *collective* insanity.

Leadership Failure #3 – hesitation in time of crisis

First Officer in charge of the *Titanic*'s bridge, William McMaster Murdoch, delayed a full thirty seconds in ordering a change of course when he was informed that the ship was in imminent danger of ramming an iceberg – which happened exactly thirty-seven seconds after the iceberg was spotted. Murdoch gave the order with just seven seconds left to impact but by that time, changing the course of the mammoth vessel was impossible.

Another ocean-liner, the *Californian*, was within sight of the *Titanic* (just six nautical miles away) when the lookout crew spotted a four-stack passenger ship that had ceased its forward motion. The crew noticed that the mysterious ship sent up numerous distress rockets at intervals, and the crew notified the *Californian*'s captain, Stanley Lord, of the ship's unusual situation. Captain Lord chose to ignore the *Titanic*'s signals, passing them off as the exuberant *celebrations* of a pleasure cruise. He had shut down his own ship's engines for the night and was unwilling to start them up again. He, likewise, neglected to awaken his communications officer so that he could canvass the area for distress calls. The *Titanic* listed and then disappeared from the horizon after two hours of observation.

In sum, poor and negligent leadership can *literally* be deadly for those who are subjected to it.

But leadership is always a double-edged sword. Good leadership can be life-giving and life-saving. Though the leadership failures of the *Titanic* will go down in history as catastrophic, we must not overlook some astounding examples of heroic leadership in the same moment of disaster.

Leadership Success #1 – sacrificial endurance

John "Jack" Phillips was the *Titanic*'s radio operator. As the ship began to sink, Captain Smith told Phillips that it was useless to keep sending out distress signals and that he should save himself and abandon ship. Phillips disregarded the order and kept sending out signals to any possible ship that could rescue them. His final message was cut short as the water entered the radio room. He risked his life to send those distress calls and barely escaped to a lifeboat, where he succumbed hours later to hypothermia before he could be rescued.

Of course, the heroism of the "band that played on" is well-known. What is not very well understood is that all eight members of the band chose to remain on board playing music to calm and console the passengers as the *Titanic* sank, and all eight band members went down with the ship. Their final song was reputed to have been, "Nearer My God to Thee."

Leadership Success #2 – never compromise

Second Officer Charles Lightoller was an experienced veteran of the sea, and he recognized immediately that the *Titanic* was in a desperate situation. His quick action freed several lifeboats that otherwise would have remained unused, which made it possible for dozens more passengers to be saved. But when one lifeboat was found to be full of men, Lightoller jumped into it and forced the men out of the boat *at gunpoint* so that women and children could be saved. He refused an order by the First Officer to board a lifeboat and was eventually sucked underwater by the sinking ship. Miraculously, the explosion of the ship's boiler as the ship went down forced Lightoller away from the sinking vessel, and he surfaced right next to one of the lifeboats he had freed. He helped keep the rickety boat afloat for the next four hours, and after seeing all the others onto the rescue boat, was the very last *Titanic* survivor to be rescued.

Leadership Success #3 – mission clarity

Fr. Thomas Byles, a forty-two-year-old English Catholic priest who was heading to New York for his brother's wedding, twice refused urgent requests that he board a lifeboat because he wanted to be available for any soul who needed his spiritual help during those moments of desperation and death. As the ship sank, the priest stood on the deck praying the Rosary as Catholics, Protestants, and Jews all knelt around him praying. Father Byle was not the only heroic clergyman on board. Scottish Evangelical Pastor John Harper was travelling with his six-year-old daughter to Chicago to preach at the church of the famed evangelist, Dwight Moody. When the *Titanic* hit the iceberg, Harper led his daughter to a lifeboat and could have gotten in because he was a widower with a small child. Instead, he kissed his daughter goodbye and ran around to every person who would listen, encouraging repentance and passionately telling others about salvation in Christ. He even gave his life jacket to a man who refused to accept the Gospel message at that late hour, commenting that the man would have another chance for salvation. Harper eventually succumbed to hypothermia in the frigid ocean with the name of Christ on his lips after presenting the message of hope to every passenger he could swim to.

Conclusion

Very few incidents in modern history show the value of leadership like the demise of the *Titanic*. The failure of leadership in so many key areas has led to a cultural image of the *Titanic* as the symbol of complete and total disaster. The preventable loss of 1,500 lives was an unmitigated tragedy, but it is not the only important truth we can derive from that sad day. The little-known stories of the unsung heroes whose principled leadership kept the disaster from reaching even greater proportions are the real leadership lessons of the *Titanic.*

Leadership is a double-edged sword: we bank on it when it is present and lament it when it is absent. Most of the time, however, we do not even think about it and presume that someone will always be there, carrying the heavy torch of responsibility into the dark night for the safety and wellbeing of people. The work of leadership is often high-profile, stress-filled, and impactful, but more often than not, it is the stuff of our regular lives. "Normal" people in all walks of life like you and me are the leaders who keep things going and perform many helpful services for our fellow humans. This is to say that leaders are like the plumber down the street whose shop you drive by every day without noticing it; he's there, but he's mostly invisible – until you have a leaky pipe.

In the following chapters, we will address five dimensions of leadership to familiarize ourselves with one of the most critical but often hidden elements of human culture that makes our world a better place in which to live: effective leadership.

The Leadership/Management Dance

There is a fundamental difference between the skills and mindsets of leaders versus managers, even though there are also many areas of overlap between the two. Leadership and management are a mesh of skills that cannot be separated; they can only be distinguished. Here's my first quick attempt at the distinctions:

- Leadership is the sum total skill set needed to take an organization's mission outward, to the world, where the mission causes life-transforming change.

- Management is the skill set needed to assure the mission's inward support so that it endures into the future and functions efficiently.

A leader's overall objectives are influence and impact; a manager's goal is efficiency. Leadership skills are directed toward marshalling human resources for action like a field lieutenant calls the platoon together and leads them into battle. Management skills are directed toward maximizing the collective capabilities of an organization like the staff sergeant who prepares the troops and makes sure they're equipped for warfare. I'll have more to say on that military analogy below.

Probably the best summary statement that was ever made on the subject came from the undisputed authority on the management profession, Peter Drucker. He made this distinction in his famous book, *The Effective Executive*: "Management is doing things right; leadership is doing the right things."[1] Because both of these functions are essentially arts rather than sciences, it is best to use a series of images to capture the nuances of the interplay between the two, *the dance,* if you will:

Leadership...	Management...
...focuses on who, what, and why	...concentrates on how
...sees the forest	...focuses on the trees
...gazes out over the horizon	...looks down for the icebergs
...sees the world awash in color	...views things in black and white
...tends to be lavish when needed	...is inclined to be stingy/economical
...spends	...cuts
...delights in what can be done	...calculates what can't be done
...admits no upper limit	...always finds the bottom line
...is creative	...is constructive
...hears music	...hears complaints
...sees opportunities	...fixes problems
...builds coalitions	...crunches numbers
...dances in the rain along Madison Avenue like a smiling Gene Kelly.	...maneuvers carefully like a stock trader on Wall Street.

---

[1]   Peter F. Drucker, *The Effective Executive,* New York: Harper and Row, 1967.

The complementarity, or overlap, between the two skill sets is usually found in each individual manager or leader. One skill set usually predominates in every individual, which can be related to his temperament and personality, but I have found that it is extremely rare for a person to be very proficient in *both* skill sets. The skills flow out of different worldviews and take time to develop into a person's individual leadership or management character. They are oriented to complementary, but different, objectives, and very few people have the capacity, or time, to pursue both.

Still, effective performers in their respective fields strive to develop both sets of skills to some degree, while recognizing that one set will always be dominant and related to their personal mindset, while the other set will be necessary for their coordination with others in work life and common projects. Leaders need management skills and managers need leadership skills to be fully professional in their approach to their missions.

A friend of mine once told me the story of a Marine Corps Staff Sergeant who was leading a group of newly-minted second lieutenants on a cleanup drill in their encampment during their first days at The Basic School (Marine officer training). The position of sergeant is the quintessential management position in any military organization, but this particular sergeant's *leadership* skills were forever burned into my friend's mind because, on that day, the lower-ranking Marine turned a routine duty of trash cleanup with his officer-trainees into a war exercise.

Technically, the Sergeant could not give orders to the officers, but he could *lead* them; so he divided the larger group into several smaller fire teams, assigned each team its objective for conquering a hill of garbage (in case you haven't noticed, Marines like to take hills), and established communication lines to give him updates on the progress of their war on trash. Not only were the young Marine officers motivated by a war game and cleaned up the field in record time, but they learned a valuable leadership lesson in that manufactured theatre of battle. The best warriors have both leadership and management skills that they put to good use in fulfilling their objectives, whatever those objectives may be. The Staff Sergeant would always be a manager in the military system, but he also knew how to lead men.

On the other hand, leaders must be intimately aware of the issues and concerns of managers and need to have some savvy in that area in order to partner with their managers in seeking solutions to complex problems. After the first successful launch of his Falcon 9 rocket in September of 2013, Elon Musk, the mercurial leader of Tesla and SpaceX, gave an interview in which he described in minute detail the workings of his rocket and why it had been successful. He had overseen just about every detail of the rocket's production process because so much of his company's fortunes depended on a successful launch. Some have accused Musk of being a micromanager – and he may be – but he is essentially a leader who has a load of technical skill to back up his endeavors. In the face of that criticism, I am reminded of what my old basketball coach used to say: "Son, we don't argue with success."

A leader needs real management ability because the ultimate leadership skill is the management of human resources, i.e., people. A good manager, likewise, has to have real leadership skills in order to motivate people to do the work and channel their skills into an efficient operation, à la the Marine Staff Sergeant. Yet, the respective skill sets remain distinct and dominant for leaders and managers, and the *individual* must blend them for effective performance.

The success of *organizations* too lies in finding that delicate balance between leadership and management within its walls. In the work of a team, this balance can be likened to two people riding a tandem bike. The leader takes the front position with the moveable handle bars to steer the bike while the manager sits in back with the fixed handlebars and provides pedal power. When they first hop on the bike, there is a period of awkwardness and instability that requires their mutual coordination and effort to stay upright, but when they reach a certain equilibrium where their coordinated efforts hurl them forward in synch, the riding smoothes out and the miles seem to pass without a hitch. Two minds thinking about the task and two bodies pedaling together make for a stronger effort. If you think about it, it is kind of like a dance.

Any complex organism lives and thrives through the coordination of its many parts, and no single part can carry out all the necessary functions. The leader's greatest challenge is to assemble all the parts of an organization for a common purpose to achieve goals outside itself, while the manager's challenge is to bring all the working parts together into an efficient instrument for channeling energy and resources to accomplish those objectives. It is sometimes true that in smaller organizations the leaders also have to be the managers and vice versa, but in all cases, large or small, the leadership and management skills are distinct even if they are not separate.

This manual is primarily about the things that make leaders effective in the non-profit sector. It is a world that requires the best leaders because its objectives are so vital for the wellbeing of people. Peter Drucker clarifies that non-profits "do something very different from either business or government. Business supplies, either goods or services. Government controls.... The 'non-profit' institution neither supplies goods or services nor controls. Its 'product' is neither a pair of shoes nor an effective regulation. Its product is a changed human being."[2] Those of us who have been in the non-profit business for years know how

---

[2] Peter Drucker, *Managing the Non-Profit Organization: Principles and Practices* (New York: HarperBusiness, 1992), xiv.

satisfying it can be to be part of a world-changing mission, and we thank God that we are called into the tangible service of people with all their human and spiritual needs. Perhaps for that reason alone I've put this book together because I believe non-profit leadership is one of the most important institutions of our time.

Chapter 1

Core Leadership Principles

1. Prayer Is the Strength of the Mission

2. You Incarnate the Mission

3. Define Success For Your Mission And Your People

4. People Will Follow Only Those Who Give Them Hope

5. Don't Be Afraid To Ask For a Sacrificial Buy-In

6. Ask Them How You're Doing

7. The Primordial Temptation

8. Beat the Perennial Catch-22

A successful man is one who can lay a firm foundation
with the bricks that others have thrown at him.
~David Brinkley

1. *Prayer Is the Strength of the Mission*

We must begin with the most important thing, perhaps the *only* thing that is truly indispensable for someone who leads a faith-based mission: prayer. I want you to hear the words of Jesus Christ clearly: "Without me you can do nothing" (John 15:5). He meant what He said. If you wish to be an effective leader in a non-profit mission, you will take these words of our Lord literally and realize that your human efforts are *necessary*, yes, *but not sufficient* to conquer kingdoms and root out evils that afflict the human community we are called to serve.

When one of her inquisitors asked St. Joan of Arc why God should need an army to accomplish His plans, she replied, "We will do the fighting, and God will supply the victory." Now, that's a response of a saint but also the attitude of a practical woman of faith who knows that her personal efforts can only get her so far in her mission. This Joan of Arc effectively ended the Hundred Years War – the longest war in history – when she was only nineteen years old. That's what you call having a lot to show for your efforts; that's also how powerful the prayer of a saint is to any kind of missionary work.

Prayer alone, which taps into the power of God, can create the climate of grace that makes all human efforts bear fruit in both material changes and in the transformation of souls. A faith-based leader simply cannot do without it. Don't give prayer a secondary priority and do not ever fall into the common delusion that "your work is your prayer." Work is work, and prayer is prayer. People sometimes fuse the two together to justify skimping on prayer. Don't do that. I am a strong advocate of praying in, through, with, before, during and after work, but don't call your work your prayer. They are distinct realms of human vitality.

Yes, it's *always* difficult to take time out of a busy schedule to "go to your inner room, close the door, and pray" (Matthew 6:6) as Jesus taught. It will never get easier to make that sacrifice of the most precious commodity we need to do our work – time. But if you don't take time for regular prayer in your day and week, your mission will suffer, not to mention your soul! Skimping on prayer is like neglecting your 401(k) payments. What happens to your retirement later on in life if you don't make regular payments *now*? Prayer has a cumulative effect on your mission which, like leadership, is often only noticed when it is absent.

You must also prioritize prayer for your people. Let them know that your mission succeeds in direct proportion to the strength of prayer being offered by the people doing the mission. Soon after Mother Teresa of Calcutta founded the Missionaries of Charity, she was challenged by her sisters to increase the amount of prayer in the chapel each day. She initially resisted this request with the common notion that they had many urgent commitments and couldn't afford to take even more time out of their busy schedules for prayer beyond their already substantial prayer schedule. Yet, she relented to her sisters' requests and began asking her sisters to spend *two hours* each day in prayer in the chapel before the Blessed Sacrament. That's what you call a serious prayer commitment!

From that point on, however, the Missionaries of Charity seemed to come alive in their mission and exponentially increased in numbers. They offered the poor something that so many other humanitarian organizations could not provide. As their name states, they gave the very life and love of God – charity – to the poor, which suffering people need much more than care packages. Their name also states their core identity which, like yours, is missionary. Prayer is the foundation of everything you do.

It is challenging for a faith-based leader to ask his associates to make prayer a regular part of their day. He does it mostly by persuasion; he constantly reminds his people that prayer is like the breath of life for their mission. Most people who participate in a faith-based mission will readily admit that prayer is important, but few make it the *primary* source of sustenance for their mission. But it is that for the leader. Spiritual ideals wane over time, especially in the hard press of responsibilities, the heat of battle, or the time of crisis, and it is the leader's work to keep the fires of prayer burning inside the organization, to constantly remind and teach his associates how essential prayer is to the survival and flourishing of the mission.

A leader may feel a bit unworldly or pious by always insisting on prayer, but that is what a leader has to do in a faith-based mission. He has to form his colleagues in habits of prayer to the point that when he forgets to pray, they turn to him and say, "Hey, when are we going to pray?" or "We can't do this without prayer. Let's stop now and pray," and similar phrases.

You may get complaints and eye rolls from time to time, but let them come. Your people must grow to expect that their leader will always be praying. They will in turn become forces of prayer themselves for the sustenance of the mission. Do not settle for mediocrity in prayer, an approach that's "good enough." Prayer is the wellspring at which your people drink for their own missionary zeal and strength.

Let us sum up what prayer does for any apostolate, any faith-based mission, any charitable work or non-profit organization and its workers:

- It sanctifies the souls of the people who pray and gives them spiritual strength to continue doing the mission;

- It creates a climate of grace so that your workers become *fruitful* in a spiritual sense and *effective* in a material sense;

- It prevents your missionary endeavors from becoming just another work of philanthropy.

Take your motivation to pray from the Archangel Raphael in the Book of Tobit: "Bless God and give him thanks before all the living for the good things he has done for you, by blessing and extolling his name in song. Proclaim before all with due honor the deeds of God, and do not be slack in thanking him" (Tobit 12:6). Amen to that.

2. *You* Incarnate *the Mission*

The idea that *the person in charge* represents the mission in a special way is at least as old as St. Paul, who said something that seems shocking to modern ears: "Imitate me as I imitate Christ" (1 Corinthians 11:1). We tend to think that such a claim lacks humility, but St. Paul's invitation did not come from an arrogant heart. It came from an understanding of how people work and live. Whether they admit it or not, people look for models to help them conduct their lives. They feel their own weaknesses deeply and want a strong person's strength to guide them. They easily adopt heroes, mentors, and role models, and willingly look to them as benchmarks for their ambitions.

You may know the story of the humble clergyman who made it into the *Canterbury Tales*. Even though we don't know the cleric's name, his simple, holy, focused life of charity so impressed the pilgrim Chaucer that six hundred years later we are still hearing about him: "There was a good man of religion, too / A country parson, poor, I warrant you / But rich he was in holy thought and work." (*Canterbury Tales*, Prologue, "The Parson.") I doubt that someone will be using *my* life as an example for anyone else six hundred years from now, but

Chaucer saw a full-blown leader with a mission of service in that simple country parson, and he wrote about it for posterity. You never know how the powerful impression of your example will carry on after you are gone.

The leader of a faith-based organization embraces his mission with the singular purpose of promoting the Gospel message or works of charity and human development. People need to see in you someone who *lives* what he believes. Hold that privilege of serving a holy mission in your hands with fear and trembling. *Incarnate* the mission for them in a very concrete sense. The mission is a living, holy thing, not an impersonal 501(c)(3) organization. Live every aspect of the mission to the greatest extent of your ability. Peter Drucker highlights how leadership competence is necessary for the good of the cause you serve:

> In the nonprofit agency, mediocrity in leadership shows up almost immediately... You can't be satisfied...with doing adequately as a leader. You have to do exceptionally well, because your agency is committed to a cause. You want people as leaders who take a great view of the agency's functions, people who will take their roles seriously – not themselves seriously.[1]

While no leader can be expected to carry out every function of the organization, you, as leader, are the *prime missionary* of a missionary organization. You are the first teacher and promoter of your prophetic cause. You are ready to answer all questions about the organization's functions and life because you have the mission in your heart and soul. You have an intimate knowledge of your founder and founding principles or charism. You spend time with those employees and long-time supporters who bear the institutional memory of the organization and its history.

[1]   Peter F. Drucker, *Managing the Non-Profit Organization: Principles and Practices* (New York: HarperBusiness, 1992), 17.

You know the organization's flaws and failings but have an intuitive grasp of what makes it tick and how God uses it to change the world. In short, you, the person at the top, are immersed in the mystery of the organization more than anyone else associated with it, including Board members who do not (should not) involve themselves in the day-to-day operation of the mission.

Additionally, and most importantly, the leader "knows his sheep" in a way that no one else can. An organization is not an impersonal set of righteous activities; it's *people*. In time you get to know *everyone* in the organization and know them well (at least those who run small or modest-sized organizations). You are the leader, the shepherd, of your people. You are the one they look to as the standard-bearer of how things are supposed to run in the mission. You incarnate the mission for them. That is not arrogance. It is a privilege and also a cross you will carry as long as you hold that blessed office.

3. *Define Success for Your Mission and Your People*

The people who follow your leadership want to know the fundamental terms of the mission and where it is taking them. Furthermore, they need to know whether or not their efforts are actually making a difference, and how. They usually can't define that for themselves; they are parts of a whole and don't always have the "big picture" view of the organization or mission as the leader does. Defining and clarifying those things for them is a main function of leadership. The role of staff and co-workers is loyalty, hard work, and fervor for a cause. The role of leaders is vision and guidance that will help them persevere in the mission through thick and thin. It is not prosaic to say that both your people and your supporters are looking for something to inspire them and marshal their tremendous energies into efforts that will truly give them a feeling of accomplishment and significance. But they have to know what they're getting into and how they can interpret their efforts.

You must therefore help them to visualize not only what the mission is but also what a *successful* mission is. You define success for them. All who participate in the organization's mission do so based on their ideals, but to be relevant and effective members of a mission, they need more than idealism. The mission itself needs someone to adapt its perennial message to the changing circumstances of the day, and the leader has to tell his people how to do that. He has to define what constitutes a true victory.

Do you know how Western Europe recovered and rebuilt itself from the devastation of the Second World War? It was primarily through the leadership talents of four men: Robert Schumann and Jean Monnet of France, Alcide de Gasparri of Italy, and Konrad Adenauer of Germany. These visionary leaders decided that there was nothing to be gained by nurturing historic animosities and pointing the finger of blame at each other. They determined that even a spirit of generous cooperation between their countries would be insufficient to bring Europe back. Only *integration* – the fusion of their countries' common interests – would rebuild their continent. To that end they laid the groundwork of the European Union and inspired their peoples to work toward that goal, even as they were digging out of the rubble of war.[2]

Having a clear vision of the future matters in leadership, but unfortunately, many leaders get so bogged down in the minutiae of running an organization that they forget to inspire people with a larger picture. Alexandre Havard notes that:

---

[2]   Alexandre Havard, *Virtuous Leadership: An Agenda for Personal Excellence* (Chicago: Scepter Publishers, Inc., 2007), 4-5. In his book, Havard chose not to address the complex Brexit issues and the ways in which the leaders of the modern European Union have betrayed the vision of its founders.

A leader, to one degree or another, is a dreamer. Parents have dreams for their children, teachers have dreams for their students, managers have dreams for their employees and politicians have dreams (as opposed to ideological fantasies) for their people.

Whether they lead many or few, leaders are always original, even though their dreams may involve traditional content. Leaders are adept at casting received wisdom in a new light, revealing its continued relevance to contemporary circumstances.[3]

The truth is that a leader must relentlessly tell his people what success looks like and help them visualize how their efforts will contribute to that ultimate objective. He works directly with them to find creative ways to bring that about. Many of a leader's best ideas come from feedback from his people "in the trenches", and from dialogue with others outside the organization who have a stake in the mission. Yet, you, as leader, have the predominant defining role for the mission. Your perspective about what constitutes "success" in this mission matters more to them than any other formulation. They may never read the glossy goals and objectives section of your company's prospectus. *Your* opinions will help them see the value of their sacrifices and will sustain them through times of hardship and drudgery.

Keep in mind that you may not be able to frame "results" for a non-profit endeavor in strict terms of investment and reward as do secular businesses. Mother Teresa's famous phrase applies to just about every charitable endeavor: "God has not asked us to be successful but to be faithful." There is something vital to that, which I will add to in future chapters. In our world, success is defined by the values of the Kingdom of God, and you have to remind your people of that again and again. But those are also

---

[3] Ibid., 20.

concrete realities that show up in the human scenarios which are the stuff of the non-profit mission. They can be evaluated by Gospel standards. The true success of virtually any altruistic movement lies not in numbers but in the transformation of lives and hearts.

The greatest benefit of "defining success" for people is that it is a major motivator. People don't make sustained sacrifices for abstract ideals. Nor do they always need to be reminded how much success their competition or opponents have. Rather, they want good, clear definitions of *what they can do*, in the here-and-now, to effect change. Learn the skill of defining success for people and practice it at every opportunity; your people will always give you their best efforts!

4. *People Will Only Follow Those Who Give Them Hope*

The one infallible law of leadership is that people will only give their sustained loyalty and commitment to those who give them hope. Inspirational leadership is the only kind of leadership that has any lasting effect on the world. Many leaders are zealous and talented. A few are brilliant and creative. Some are ruthless and extremely efficient. Yet, the one quality that defines an *effective* leader is his ability to focus people on the basic desires of the human heart and inspire them to change a tainted world. How many zealous leaders lose sight of this fundamental principle because they get overly comfortable in their positions or become too worried about making ends meet? It is almost guaranteed that if your leadership inspires people at some very basic level, you will not have to worry about making ends meet.

For all his faults as a man and as a neophyte political leader, John F. Kennedy was about as inspirational a leader as we've had in America. He had a distinct personal charisma for sure, but more importantly, he inspired people to work for the common objective of marshalling our phenomenal American ingenuity into the world's best space program. He claimed forthrightly that America was going to put a man on the moon by the end of the decade. He was not presenting his countrymen with an option. His vision was specific and ambitious, as dreams should be. As we know, Kennedy never got to see that dream fulfilled, but he inspired a whole generation of talented men and women to put this hopeful vision into effect.

Think about the advances in technology that have emerged from that vision! To cite just one symbolic example of the technological tsunami that flowed out of the space program: it is said that a single smartphone that billions of people carry in their pockets today contains more raw computing power than the Apollo 11 Spacecraft that put Neil Armstrong and Buzz Aldrin on the surface of the moon. Kennedy's promise "of landing a man on the Moon and returning him safely to Earth before this decade is out" drove the whole effort. That is effective leadership in the art of hope.

The same can be said of leaders of charitable organizations of any stripe. The best leaders do not always have Kennedy-esque charm, but all effective leaders tell people they can make some kind of tangible difference in the world and then show them how to do it. They also create a context in which their people can work together to create that distinct change in the world, a change larger than any individual can make on his own. Hence, the three elements of inspirational leadership give your people great confidence for the future:

- giving people *meaning* (an inspiring, well-articulated mission)

- showing them how to translate that meaning into *action* (defining success) and

- creating a *system* for cooperation to effect those changes in the world (we'll address this in the next few chapters)

Remember: people will only follow those who give them hope.

5. *Don't Be Afraid to Ask for a Sacrificial Buy-In*

A very excellent (but not at all Kennedy-esque) leader once told me that his organization doesn't pay people to be part of the action; rather, *people pay to join the action* created by his organization. He wasn't referring to money. He was referring to *sacrifices* – time, talents, effort, etc. In other words, leaders know that there is a buy-in aspect to any successful movement or organization. An undertaking that taps into something noble in the human spirit is a movement that costs something to join, but is also, for that very reason, its own reward. Learn the lesson of buy-in from all good leaders.

An altruistic movement calls people to a heroism that enlivens them at a very deep level. Its leaders are only successful to the extent that they ask people for a sacrificial buy-in to the cause. The leader believes this maxim: the greater the sacrifice, the greater the reward. Jesus told people that the Kingdom of God was the "pearl of great price" (Matthew 13:46) for which a man was willing to sell everything he owned. Your cause too is the most precious cause on earth. The buy-in to it can be very costly at times but also full of blessings. You've made the buy-in, haven't you? Why not ask others to do the same?

Chilean saint, Fr. Alberto Hurtado (1901-1952), was fond of saying that "it is proper to the noblest souls to discover the most urgent necessity of the day and consecrate themselves to it." There is something about "consecrating oneself to a cause" that rings true for endeavors that address human suffering and needs. Even causes whose purpose is not crisis management as such, but the advancement of knowledge, wellbeing, technology, etc., are enhancing human life in some way. Not every cause has to do with life-and-death realities, but most charitable organizations, knowingly or not, base their mission on Fr.

Hurtado's "most urgent necessity of the day" rationale: we are making the world a better place to live in – today.

Peter Drucker said that "one of the great strengths of a non-profit organization is that people don't work for a living, they work for a cause (not everybody, but a good many). That also creates a tremendous responsibility for the institution, to keep the flame alive, not to allow work to become just a 'job.'"[4] He's right. The notion that *the cause is a flame* to be kept burning is the inspirational work of leadership.

As a leader of actual flesh-and-blood people, you must be aware that achieving a sacrificial buy-in is usually a *process*, not a one-time decision. That is more in keeping with human nature, which doesn't persevere easily in difficult things. There is a three-stage trajectory of enthusiasm-disillusionment-solid commitment in the rare few who persevere in a serious human-betterment cause. It goes like this:

The neophyte enters the arena full of naïve zeal to change the world, only to find that the world is the way it is because some serious vested interests (political, economic, or ideological) *want it to stay that way.* He then has to overcome his disillusionment about the impenetrable walls that stand in the way of any change. He may even be persecuted for his convictions and find that his foes may be very organized and sometimes very powerful. He discovers, to his chagrin, that his enemies or competitors don't give up without a fight and that slothful human habits and institutions don't change easily. Finally, after much soul-searching and only with God's grace, he makes a humble assent to a lifelong commitment to have some real impact on the larger context of the problem (the culture, the institutions, the hearts of people, etc.) Only then does he allow the Lord to show him where and how he can do that most effectively.

---

4   Drucker, *Non-Profit*, 150.

About one in a hundred true-blood warriors for a cause will follow that trajectory to end-stage commitment. Even most good-hearted people do not persevere in their commitments against immovable objects, and some just get burned out or *taken out* by life's inevitable crises and other circumstances. But that one-in-a-hundred committed soul, somewhere along the way, will have been inspired by a real leader who showed him that winning the battle was both necessary and possible. Someone once defined "winning" for him. That same leader asked him for a sacrificial buy-in, which crystallized his serious commitment to the cause.

I once met a Catholic priest who told me his inspiring vocation story. As a teenager he was struggling with the question of what to do with his life. He had all the career possibilities ahead of him that American society could offer, and he was talented enough to take advantage of any one of them. Yet, he felt uneasy about whether he should dedicate his life to marriage and family or to service of the Kingdom in a religious vocation. After telling his dilemma to his pastor, the priest told him to go into the church and read the next Sunday's readings in the missalette, and the Word of God would clarify things for him. So the young man dutifully opened the Gospel passage for the next Sunday which read: "As [Jesus] was walking by the Sea of Galilee, he saw two brothers, Simon who is called Peter, and his brother Andrew, casting a net into the sea; they were fishermen. He said to them, 'Come after me, and I will make you fishers of men.' At once they left their nets and followed him" (Matthew 4:18-20). "That's it!" cried the young man. "I've found my calling. I want to be a fisher of men!"

His vocation had two inspirational leadership moments: 1/ the Lord who called him to an inspirational life of service and 2/ the young man's pastor who magnified the voice. (The pastor had obviously prepared his sermon to preach on those readings the next Sunday!) In time, that young man went through his own process of disillusionment and decision which brought him to ordination to become the fruitful minister of the Gospel he is today.

Many people are asked to take over positions for which they feel inadequately prepared. But while training and personal abilities certainly contribute to leadership success, these are not the most essential elements. The most critical leadership trait for persevering in a cause is the attitude of *godly courage,* which pushes beyond our cultural reluctance to "inconvenience" people and asks for a sacrificial buy-in from others to fulfill some great need. The leader is one who believes so strongly in the nobility and truth of his cause that he develops a *fearlessness* about asking people to join him. He makes no apologies for his convictions and even wonders why the whole world is not on his side in his battle to end all battles. How blessed is the leader who overcomes his fear of inconveniencing others and asks people to make sacrifices that, in turn, will transform the world and lead them to Heaven. That's a pretty good trade-off.

6. *Ask Them How You're Doing*

The famous Fr. Richard John Neuhaus, civil rights marcher, human rights advocate, author of a dozen books, founder of *First Things* magazine, and popular public speaker, was a leader in every sense. One of his many startling leadership habits was to ask his less experienced co-workers two questions to which they were invited to give totally candid answers: "What am I *doing* that I should not be doing?" and "What am I *not doing* that I should be doing?"

According to his co-workers, Fr. Neuhaus never disputed their answers or got defensive if they sounded critical or mentioned something he was not aware of in their assessment. He solicited their feedback for a good reason: he knew that he could not see himself or his actions objectively. He needed *other sets of eyes* looking at him and evaluating him from different perspectives – honestly and candidly, in a spirit of mutual cooperation – and he was honest enough to ask for it. He allowed their feedback to shape him into the kind of leader God wanted him to be.

The flaw of most leaders is the tendency to retreat into a sort of institutional isolation that shuns accountability for their actions and words. Whether consciously or not, many believe they do not *need* accountability or do not need to deliberately ask for it. Yet, without it, a person cannot be a full or effective leader. A leader's performance is always subject to scrutiny, whether he likes it or not, whether or not he asks for it. In the end, all leaders, like all souls, must stand before the Just Judge and account for their leadership. Jesus was very clear that "there is nothing hidden that will not be revealed" (Luke 8:17), and that applies most directly to Christian leadership of any type. Getting hidden things out into the open through objective feedback, a third-party view of your work, is as good a way as any to prepare for that Final Judgment.

Former New York City Mayor, Ed Koch, used to walk through crowds of fawning admirers and, with his sly smile and sing-song delivery, ask them, "How'm I doin'?!" – to which they, of course, would *always* answer in the affirmative! But that is not real feedback. Honest and accurate feedback is also not a matter of public opinion polls. Rather, it is a matter of a leader's attitude, which values the ideas and opinions of others close to him as "mirrors" of truth and seeks to know how his decisions, attitudes, and leadership style impact the world. This is not a game of image-building. It's training in humility which destroys the temptation to hide from accountability. It's also risky business because we may not always like what we hear and may be deeply challenged by it.

Find creative ways to canvass people for feedback. Sometimes it is as direct and transparent as the Neuhaus method or a rigorous company evaluation process. Other times a leader gets feedback *indirectly* through casual conversations with co-workers and volunteers, the latter of whom may be more candid with you because their jobs don't depend on keeping the boss happy! You can even garner feedback through anonymous surveys (you'd be surprised at what you learn when people don't have to put their names to something.)

Believe it or not, our enemies can also teach us many important things about ourselves, and we would be very wise to listen to their perspective, however distorted we may judge it. Our foes at the very least present another view of ourselves that is entirely out of our comfort zones. Enemies have a way of honing in on our greatest weaknesses, and that's not a bad thing for a leader to see. Whatever the source, feedback on job performance and policies is necessary for us to develop the habits of honesty and tested leadership. Without objective evaluation and feedback, you cannot grow as a leader.

The real danger to a leader is thinking that very few people have anything to offer him. This attitude is deadly to the leader's integrity and working relationships. Drucker, again, once commented that most of the leaders he had met in his long career of studying leaders were "neither born nor made. They were self-made."[5] That's a pretty good assessment of what it takes to reach leadership success in any sector. You are the product of your own plan of personal development, as well as many other influences and objective factors, such as evaluations and feedback, and your willingness to follow up on them. More importantly, by asking others how you are doing and subjecting yourself to the test of human judgment, you eventually become the kind of leader God wishes you to be.

---

[5] Ibid., 21.

7. *The Primordial Temptation*

The first temptation of the leader who has a life-giving mission—from the Red Cross to the lowliest church community—is to *strangle the mission to feed the organization*. That is, the leader, even if not as a deliberate act, can "use" the mission as a pretext for perpetuating the institution. But it has to be the other way around: the mission sustains the organization. Bureaucracies exist to perpetuate themselves. Sometimes non-profit organizations do too, but they shouldn't. There is nothing more antithetical to a missionary organization than for it to become a bureaucracy.

Organizations with employees have to make payroll, they have to pay bills and meet increasing and burdensome compliance costs, etc. Most organizations that ask for donations are cash-strapped, both because of the ebb and flow of charitable giving and because the needs are so great that there never seems to be enough cash to meet them. I know the stress of that dynamic well: I've been immersed in it for three decades. This gives rise to the leader's primordial temptation to sacrifice mission objectives *just to keep the institution running*. The demands of cash flow can be inordinate at times: organizations tend to eat up cash like the insatiable Pac-Man.[6] So train yourself to spot the four common ways leaders give in to this primordial temptation:

Skewing the Programs/Operations Balance

Non-profit monitoring websites such as "Charity Navigator" and "GuideStar" generally consider an 80/20 ratio to be a

---

[6]   An ancient, first generation video game in the '70s that featured a ball-like monster with an enormous mouth rushing through the corridors of a labyrinth eating everything in sight. The player's challenge was to keep him from swallowing the bomb! (I loved the *chomping* sound of the ball as it ate up its opponents.)

healthy Programs (mission) vs. Operations (administration and fundraising) balance, although this index is by no means the only factor used to rate an organization's effectiveness.[7] The ratio is meant to be an objective indicator of institutional health. The right Programs/Ops balance is fundamental to being able to honestly tell donors that *your expenditures reflect your mission priorities.* Those organizations that progressively sink more money into their operations and self-promotional schemes usually do not survive long. Keep the balance; if you lose it, get back to it.

Mission Entertainment

Organizations sometimes "play to an audience" in order to ratchet up donations from one sector of their donor base and assure a better cash flow. If this tendency is left unchecked for very long, the mission can lose its substance and devolve into a sort of "mission entertainment" gig of constantly doing superficial things that have a tenuous relation to the real mission. Every organization must have and keep strong constituencies, but this kind of thing is usually geared to keeping a particular audience happy, getting attention, or appealing to a vocal partisan group who will keep donating to the institution only when it advocates their specific cause. The organization can turn into a sort of propaganda machine that generates enough attention and money to perpetuate the institution but is empty of any *real* impact. If you have had the misfortune to land on the mailing list of an organization of this type, ask yourself how many "Surveys," "Urgent Email Alerts – **Must Take Action Now!**" and dramatically-worded "Congressional Petitions" to change outcomes actually *do* change anything. It's all mission entertainment. Don't imitate it.

---

[7] Note: churches do not appear on these registers because they are not required by the IRS to file 990 forms, which track revenues.

Fudging the Numbers and Perceptions

The temptation to increase cash flow at the expense of the mission can even expand into fudging the numbers and perceptions of your organization. What this means is that an organization can present its mission in public pronouncements in more flattering terms than it really deserves. Leaders may *creatively* use charts, campaigns, slogans, statistics, etc. to impress their soft donors or divert public attention away from their true activities rather than actually account for their resources.

Here's an extreme example. The truly wicked Planned Parenthood is actually a non-profit organization! They have based their public image on the perception that they provide services to needy women. But their *claims* to provide numerous fundamental services related to women's health needs – such as breast cancer screenings – far outweighs the reality and percentage of these services in their budgets. Their propaganda does one thing very effectively though: it serves to draw attention away from their one key service that has very negative branding, namely, being the largest abortion provider in the world. This is an extreme example, but it is not by any means the only example of obfuscating the numbers and perceptions to create an aura of nobility that doesn't hold up to moral scrutiny.

The possibilities for subtle deception in the pursuit of funds, attention or prestige are enormous and need to be checked by regular operations audits and honest evaluations of the public relations of the organization. A sincere examination of conscience to account for the mission should be a regular part of every organization that solicits funds from God's generous people.

Mission Compromise

Most leaders, at some point in their careers, will have to decide whether to water down the mission/message for the sake of economic survival or bite the bullet and stay true to their core values, come what may. Sometimes the challenge comes in the form of the wrath of a big donor who threatens to withdraw donations because he wants your mission to continue implementing *his* expectations. This kind of person has not really paid attention to the full and logical implications of your mission. Donor wrath may also cut the opposite way: donors may not want new leadership or any type of change from what they thought they built through their donations. These are very real concerns, and a leader should never take complaints like this lightly. However, you must also never allow yourself or your organization to be held hostage by them. Handle each one of these carefully and personally. But do not compromise the essence of your mission.

When I took over a failing non-profit in the early 2000s I had to deal with a group of angry donors who had withdrawn their donations and made a very public show of their complaints. I judged that their complaints were in some measure valid, so I personally met with the group and heard many of their expressions of anxiety that the mission they had donated to for so long was going in the wrong direction, away from what it was founded to do. I assured them that the founding missionary spirit was alive and well with the new leadership and then clarified for them how I intended to take the organization forward. That seemed to settle things.

Nevertheless, if they had irrationally persisted in continuing the fight, I had a sheet of paper in my briefcase listing each donor's contributions over the years, and I was prepared to inform them that the total cumulative value of *all* their contributions would actually run the current organization *for only three weeks*. (One of the "donors" had once received a paycheck from the organization but had never actually made a single contribution to it!)

We are always grateful for people's contributions, but angry donors or pressure groups sometimes need a wakeup call and a sense of realism about their own importance. Mind you, I was very respectful and expressed gratitude for their gifts. But I learned quickly that there is often an inverse relationship between vocal calls for change and *actual* support. Keep that in mind.

Faith-based missions raise funds by assuring people they are out there changing the world in a dynamic way, but that assurance must be real. Your responsibility to the donors requires you to show *tangible evidence* of effective action. It's the mission that perpetuates the institution through the goodwill and donations of many people, not the other way around. Don't fall prey to the temptation to use the mission to *perpetuate* the institution – and never, ever water down your mission. That leads us to our next point.

8. *Beat the Perennial Catch-22*

Mission and money co-exist in a special symbiosis in any organization. The mission needs money to operate in the real world, but organizations don't get money unless they have a mission, right? It's the classic Catch-22.

Essentially, it means that we have to take money *away from* the mission in order to get money *for* the mission. It's as simple and stark as that. It's one of those harsh realities that every leader of a charitable organization faces abruptly upon assumption of office, particularly when an organization is a start-up or is in any type of institutional crisis. The only way to get out of the grip of this awful reality is to *take the Catch-22 bull by the horns and run it into the ground*. It's a grueling task that requires sustained sacrifice over a certain (but not necessarily long) period of time, but it's a battle that is well worth the wounds.

To defeat the Catch-22 bull, a leader has to become a fundraiser, a public relations master, an entrepreneur, and a dynamic promoter all rolled into one. We'll address these qualities in the next few chapters. These endowments are not based on personality so much as on *predictable and obtainable skills.* Nor do they belong to just one person in the organization. In smaller organizations one person may unfortunately have to shoulder most of these functions himself, but a good leader gathers together people who have these talents and forms them into a team that will help him meet these needs. While you have to be knowledgeable about fundraising techniques, you will often depend on people with professional fundraising skills to help you. The same is true for PR, communications, and promotions. We often depend on professionals.

But even if you don't have the luxury of professional fundraisers and PR people on staff, there is plenty of good advice out there about how to develop these trainable skills and a mountain of tried-and-true strategies you can implement.[8] The point is, don't wait. The *costs* of running an organization wait for no man, and they won't wait for you.

In the matter of generating capital to run your mission, there is no easy way. It's all hard. So get used to it and start fundraising today, not tomorrow. Be responsible *and creative* in asking, cajoling, begging, borrowing, (you can forego stealing), and be energetic in doing what it takes to financially sustain your mission.

Defeating the perennial Catch-22 usually requires great creativity and effort, but if *you* don't get the money to fuel your mission, no one else will step up to the plate and do it. That's leadership. It takes an adamant will, a lot of humility, and a positive, creative spirit to overcome the Catch-22 paradox. But *you* can beat the bull – if you work at it. It is literally a matter of sheer determination.

---

[8] The Fundraising Authority (www.thefundraisingauthority.com) is quite literally the greatest authority and information resource for non-profit fundraising. Likewise, the organization known simply as Nonprofit PR (www.nonprofitPR.org) offers every possible best practice for getting your message out. For further information, check out other "Web-Based Non-Profit Resources" in the Helpful Resource section at the back of this book.

Be like the bullfighter who walks confidently into the arena, looks the raging beast square in the face, flashes the red cape and says to mister bull, "Bring it." Each time you walk into the ring to take on the rushing bull, you strike the beast with those colorful but deadly spears and, *little by little,* you drain it of power, leading to its ultimate collapse. Whether for a family or an organization, providing for material needs is always difficult, but it *does* get easier. Take the responsibility squarely on your shoulders, use all the resources at your disposal, and believe beyond the shadow of a doubt that in time you *will* defeat the raging Catch-22 bull.

Conclusion

Every noble mission needs a person of strength and competence leading the charge, and your cause is no different. Be that leader who holds up the values of the movement to his co-workers and supporters; live those values; and constantly remind people of why they fight for those worthy goals. Don't make the cause into your personal campaign, though, because God can use any instrument to do His work and you – sorry to say – are as dispensable as the leaders who came before you, who are now gone. God needs leaders who do not depend on themselves too much but who try to live their faith in a heroic and inspiring way in service to others. That's the message of the Gospel, and that's why we work. Everything else is in God's hands – where it should be.

Chapter 2

Core Promotional Principles

1. Know Why the World Needs You

2. Promote the Mission With Simplicity and Clarity

3. Communicate With Boldness and Creativity

4. Inspiration, Inspiration, Inspiration

5. Be Prepared for Every Audience

6. Money Follows Mission

7. Stay Constantly in Front of Them

8. Don't Confuse Having an Audience With Having an Impact

I should be sorry if I only entertained them;
I wished to make them better.

~*George Frideric Handel*

1. *Know Why the World Needs You*

During my second week of a new job at a non-profit organization in the early 2000s, a respected mentor phoned and asked me to tell him in a few words why the world needed my organization. I'm not usually at a loss for words, but this question caught me flatfooted. I hemmed and hawed. I think I said that I needed more time to become familiar with the organization, etc. But it was clear that I had no quick answer, and he did not press me for one. It was enough for him to have planted the question in my mind and heart, knowing that it would burn there until I found an adequate answer.

After much soul-searching, observation, experience, and discussion about our mission with my co-workers, I *did* answer that question. Furthermore, I discovered that *answering that particular question for myself* was one of the milestones in my leadership learning curve. It was also one of the best things I ever did for the effective promotion of our mission.

But that dilemma is not unique to me. *Every leader* has to answer that question regarding his own mission. When we find out what makes us tick, we go forward with a much clearer sense of purpose. If we are not clear about the reason for our existence, why should anyone else be? No leader can afford to use canned slogans, hackneyed reasoning, or vague descriptions to explain his mission and organization. He can't take someone else's word for it. He has to find out for himself the true meaning of his mission and be utterly convinced that his organization is the vehicle for that righteous cause. Only then will he become its promoter *par excellence*.

The greatest enemy to the effective promotion of your cause is confusion or fuzzy thinking about the mission. To tell the public who you are is to reaffirm your core values and to purify your motivations for the work. Much of our clarity about our work is the result of repetition. We become clearer and more convinced of our mission the more we tell others about it. At times, an organization may make changes to its mission statement or update/adapt the mission to meet unforeseen challenges, but these changes are never the result of muddled thinking or shifting values. They are the result of deliberate planning and adaptation to environmental changes.

The venerable K-Mart chain (incorporated as S.S. Kresge Corporation in 1899!) was a victim of fuzzy thinking. In the 1980s, with the rise of big box discount retailers like Walmart and Target, they forgot who they were. The competition for customers looking for a broad range of "low price" consumer options was stiff, and K-Mart was looking a little like the redneck cousin of the growing family because of its Blue Light Specials (BLS) and the declining condition of its stores.

Furthermore, the BLS got a reputation in popular culture as the iconic cheap shopping promo that excited the denizens of trailer parks but that no sophisticated person would ever accept. That was just a parody. The reality was that the BLS remained the signature and most successful promotional feature of the K-Mart brand until corporate thinking became fuzzy.

Instead of cleaning up their stores and competing more efficiently in the face of the new kids on the block, Kmart leadership wallowed in an identity crisis. In 1991, attempting to get away from the hokey image and upgrade their product lines, they cancelled the familiar, *"Attention K-Mart Shoppers!"* Blue Light Special announcement that drew people to their stores, and by 2002 they were forced to declare bankruptcy. The following year they merged with Sears to stay alive, but in October of 2018 their fortunes had dramatically declined, and they filed for Chapter 11. K-Mart forgot who they were and abandoned their primary promotional asset. Cancelling the BLS was not the sole cause of bankruptcy, but it was definitely a clear contributing factor and an example of deadly corporate fuzzy thinking about their mission.

Although the "products and services" a non-profit offers are different from the corporate world, the principles of promotion remain the same. Keep fuzzy thinking about your identity at bay. Stay clear about who you are, what you do, and what makes you tick. Communicate it regularly and with passion to your stakeholders, your allies, and even your enemies, and you will convince many good souls that the world really *does* need you.

2. *Promote the Mission With Simplicity and Clarity*

Always promote the essence of your mission with simplicity and clarity. If you know *why* the world needs your organization and mission, then you should also be able to boil down *what you do* to several handy formulas to promote the mission. At any given time and for any given audience you should be able to:

- Tell them *in one paragraph* about your mission, or

- Tell them *in one summary sentence* what your mission is, or

- Tell them *in six words* what your mission is, or

- Display the essence of what you stand for in a slogan that can fit *on a coffee cup or a t-shirt.*

In our modern sound-bite culture, it is important to express your mission succinctly; the attention spans of people are atrociously short and marketing must be extremely focused. In fact, a new study by Microsoft Corporation found that the average attention span of a technology-using human being is shorter than that of a *goldfish*. Really. (To be specific,

Microsoft determined that it was 9 seconds, whereas that of a goldfish is 10.)

What this means is that you have to package your mission's identity in clear terms for people who will not normally give you the time of day. You may only have a few precious seconds to communicate your message to others in a fast-paced world. This is commonly referred to as the "elevator pitch" – the amount of time available while riding an elevator to answer the question, "So, what do you do?" Do *you* have an elevator pitch? You may need to use it tomorrow.

As a leader, you have to be ready to give a clear and cogent explanation of your mission to any audience at any time, and you have to do it with clarity and simplicity. Which is easier to interpret – the traffic light at the corner, or the million-word, ever-shifting, mammoth schedule board at Grand Central Terminal? Both communicate things. The board is a lot bigger than any traffic light, so it should be easier for people to see and read, right? No.

Promotions never work that way. They do not blast large amounts of information at people. The intricate schedule board is not a promotional instrument. It has a different function. It attempts to bring order to an amazingly complex system of moving objects – trains – that everyone has to use, but its vital messages can't be read or interpreted in an instant like the traffic light can. Nor should they.

The promotion of anything takes place by means of easily-understandable, well-packaged, clear and concise sound bites or unambiguous symbols like the traffic light. (Hint: traffic lights promote the *really good* idea of traffic safety.) It is not the communication of large amounts of information. In newsletters, talks, and publications you have the luxury of addressing more complex issues with your audiences, but not in promotions. The fascinating work of branding, logos, slogans, mottos, and sound-bite communications all belong to this realm, and you should take the art of these things seriously if you want to promote your mission.

The lesson here is that *complexity is death*. If you attempt to project too many ideas about your mission at once to your audience, you run the risk of confusion or of causing your core identity to be muddled in their minds. Your mission is utterly unique. It is that uniqueness that must receive first billing, not all the rich complexity of your organization's activities.

No one else understands your mission like you do, and your audiences need to hear it explained clearly and simply from you as its leader so they come away with a deeply-embedded image of your noble cause in their minds. On most occasions you have only one opportunity to make a good first impression. Make the best of it. The more uncluttered your presentation is, the more likely it is to stick in the mind of the potential donor.

All leaders should become familiar with the principles of *branding*. It is the art of capturing a space in the minds of people so that when they call up their "mental file" of your organization, they will see some clear image of it, distinct from all other mental files and images.[1] Companies spend mega millions on advertising for that reason. Quick: how many minutes does it take for GEICO to save you 15% on your car insurance? Anyone who has watched television for the last decade should be able to answer that question because GEICO has captured that mental space through aggressive advertising/branding with a funny, cockney-speaking spokesgecko! The GEICO gecko is one of most effective branding campaigns in the history of advertising.

Clarity is the challenge. In order for you to capture space in people's minds, you must give them clear and attractive images, uncluttered ideas, and messages that stick. These must

---

[1]   Al Ries & Jack Trout (*The 22 Immutable Laws of Marketing*, New York: Harper, 1994), 14.

be simple, true, noble, and vivid in order to make an impression. These simple promotional tools must convey your mission without confusion and exactly as you want your audiences to perceive it.

3. *Communicate With Boldness and Creativity*

As a corollary to simplicity and clarity, a leader needs to present his mission with boldness and creativity. Boldness is a *profound personal passion* about your mission. On Sunday, a congregation can easily tell if a preacher has let his beliefs touch his very soul. Sunday worshippers are often *bored stiff* by lifeless preaching which should present the most exciting truths of creation in rich imagery and zeal, but don't, because their preachers fail the boldness and creativity test. The famous motivational speaker, Zig Ziglar, once quipped that most preaching is "the art of talking in someone else's sleep"! The effective preacher/evangelizer shows that he passionately believes his message and then connects the truths of the faith with the lives of his congregants. He is the one who sways hearts. In fact, he will probably stand head and shoulders above the other preachers who just *sort of* believe in the Gospel.

I once saw a video of people who had lived their whole lives with color blindness and were one day given the gift of some glasses with special lenses that made it possible for them to see the world bathed in color *for the first time*. Needless to say, *every single one of them* broke down in tears at finally being able to see the immense beauty of the world that most of us take for granted each day.

A passionate presentation of a mission and its message is like that for people who have been accustomed to seeing black-and-white presentations their whole lives! It is a real education to watch good preachers touch lives and hearts: look at the passion of pastors like Rick Warren, Joyce Myers, Johnny Hunter, and Charles Stanley, among others. The voices of premier Catholic preachers past and present (Archbishop Fulton Sheen, Father John Corapi, Father Benedict Groeschel, Bishop Robert Barron, and others) stun with their brilliance. They are full of passion, storytelling, and zeal. No one ever left their sermons less a Christian.

There are many tools for life-changing presentations in the arsenal of effective promotions: color, pictures, numbers, stories and anecdotes, as well as dynamism, emotion, and movement in the delivery. The more creative and imaginative you are in creating a picture of your mission, the more people will pay attention to you. We live in a sound bite and visual culture so the presentations have to be vivid and convincing without being overly flashy or fake.

Your creativity in presenting your mission is limited only by your imagination. In previous generations, leaders had to appeal to the public almost exclusively through print media (newspapers, brochures, newsletters, press releases and written fundraising appeals), as well as through speeches and conferences. These remain very effective means of reaching certain audiences but are not sufficient to reach wider audiences of potential supporters today. With the Internet as our primary communications highway, leaders need to be savvy in using electronic and social media to promote their causes and organizations.

Above all, master the art of imagery and word-pictures so that the mission will become real to your audiences. Abstract concepts and explanations are a waste of time for all but the most academically-oriented audiences.

One of the best examples of bold, creative communication in the modern age is Dennis Prager's phenomenal video program with the magnificently clear name of "Prager University". Just the name gives you the mission – education, education, and more education – and the leader who made it all possible. These concise and interesting five-minute videos are visual gems with clear, colorful, and dynamic messages and imagery that bring to life the concepts of the narrator, who is usually a recognized expert on a given subject. The videos are marvels of creative and simple teachings, which also promote Prager's organization effectively.

To communicate to modern audiences well, take leaders like Prager and others who communicate with boldness and creativity and make them your models. Find out what makes them tick, discover their secrets, and then go and do the same.

4. *Inspiration, Inspiration, Inspiration*

Effective promotion is not a matter of parroting slogans. It is moving hearts. In this we imitate Our Lord, who very effectively used stories and images to teach simple people and often large audiences. Anyone who has ever heard the parables of the mustard seed, the Prodigal Son or the Good Samaritan can never forget them because of their imagery and capacity to draw on the imagination. Never underestimate the power of inspiration to move hearts.

Motivational speaker, Wes Beavis, said: "Frankly, the world doesn't need any more brilliant and talented people.... The world needs more people who have the heart to encourage and inspire others to personally grow."[2] Storytelling is an essential quality of leadership, and you should learn it well. In his creative little book called, simply, *Leadership*, Tom Peters of the McKinsey Group advises leaders to "hone your storytelling chops." He cites the Harvard psychologist Howard Gardner's insight that "a key, perhaps *the* key, to leadership is...the effective communication of a story."[3] I couldn't agree more wholeheartedly.

---

[2] Wes Beavis, *Fuel 2: Keeping You and Your Team Fired Up* (Irvine, California: Powerborn, 2010), 118.

[3] Tom Peters, *Leadership: Inspire, Liberate, Achieve* (New York: DK Publishing, Inc., 2005), 91; citing Gardner, *Leading Minds: An Anatomy of Leadership*, 78.

Start with your own people. If you are working for an altruistic cause, you will never be lacking examples of generosity and heroism in your movement. Tap the reservoir of good deeds and stories of sacrifice around you to give a human face to the mission. These stories highlight the circumstances and decisions that illustrate the value of the mission.

I remember reading in the newsletter of a crisis pregnancy center the amazing story of a blind man who wanted his wife to have an abortion. He accompanied her to the pregnancy center thinking it was the abortion clinic. The nurse brought the wife into the ultrasound room to do a scan, and her husband went with her. Of course, the blind man couldn't see the picture of the baby on the screen, so the nurse connected the Doppler to the ultrasound machine and the husband could *hear* the baby's rapid little heartbeat *in utero*. Instantly, the man broke down in tears, and that was the end of any talk about abortion.

This is heroism at its finest – both on the part of the people who changed their choice as well as the people who were there to help them – and stories like that need to be told.

Make sure to keep a file of inspiring or human interest stories that relate to your movement, even if these stories are not directly about your organization or co-workers. Never miss an opportunity to carefully document the heroics of others whose deeds may not have had wide exposure but which you can use in newsletters, motivational talks, fundraising, etc. to craft a picture of why the world needs you and your mission. There is no limit to inspiration's power: stories of heroism and generosity do more to motivate people than a hundred academic talks on "issues". They also keep the troops fighting for another day.

5. *Be Prepared for Every Audience*

As the public face of the organization, you are also its Number One Promoter. Get used to that responsibility. The singular impression that most people have of the mission usually comes from the one who leads it. Who can tell you the names of any of the other employees of Pat Robertson's Christian Broadcasting Network? It's "All Pat, all the time." Who else works for the Catholic League for Religious and Civil Rights other than the amazing Dr. Bill Donahue? There are many more employees; yet, who would know it? Father Frank Pavone's organization is called Priests for Life, but some call it *Priest* for Life because Father Pavone is the ever-present public face of the mission.

Leaders who faithfully represent their organizations understand that the public mostly draws its knowledge of their mission from the way they present it and themselves. The primary challenge for dynamic leaders is to continue to represent the organization without allowing it to become an extension of their own egos. The leader exists for the good of the organization, not the other way around.

You must therefore be able to present a coherent message to diverse audiences and not be afraid to branch out to groups that are outside the comfort zone of true believers or like-minded warriors. A very smart friend of mine once wrote a plan to help leaders remain relevant to a wide range of audiences. He said:

> *Write and master three types of speeches/presentations. One speech is to make money, "both cash and caché," and it should be something smart and entertaining and on point.*

> *The second set of speeches, presentations, retreats includes "high-value" addresses designed to be delivered before major interest groups and universities, enabling the reform-minded leader to project the brand and program of reform in tough days.*

> *The third speech, of course, is the "stump speech" that explains and motivates people to get involved with the program of reform. To this I would add the regular*

authoring of essays, op-eds, and other written materials that keep you "out there" and intellectually engaged in the reform project.

The best thing a leader can do—and as soon as possible—is to get professional coaching to help him evaluate and improve his public presentations. You need to invest money and time in this skill set. Set down your *foundation as a communicator* early on in your time at the helm, and then you can refine your presentations as time goes on. You will eventually need to adapt them to more diverse audiences. Rome wasn't built in a day, and you can't expect to have the speaking savvy of a veteran in your first year; yet, the time to begin work on your speaking repertoire is now.

Too many leaders, even those with great experience, unfortunately "wing it" when it comes to talks and important presentations (which, for clergy, certainly includes the genre of sermons!)

Let me say categorically: *Never do that.* Your people deserve more.

On the other hand, some effective speakers give the *impression* that they are speaking off the cuff or being spontaneous in their talks, but their casual manner is usually meant to disarm people and open them up to the message. They are never making it up as they go. These experts have spent many hours in the preparation of their message, and their casual but effective manner of communicating with certain audiences is actually the fruit of great preparation. If you saw them in front of a different audience the following week, their presentation would be different, tailored to that audience, but it would have the same spontaneous feel to it.

The motivated leader who wants to communicate well has many tools available to help him. You and your organization should always have a set of talking points on all current issues of concern to your mission as well as message management guidelines crafted carefully with co-workers to establish consistent positions on your particular issues.

Media training is also critical to the leader's professional approach to modern communications. Giving radio and television interviews is a must for ongoing promotion of your mission, and in this area you need to have good coaching and feedback, before, during, and after your appearances and presentations, if possible. Most broadcast media outlets are starving for interviews with dynamic leaders, and it is never hard to get media attention, at least at the local level.

You may also wish to develop a long-term media strategy for promotion of your message and mission to wider audiences. This plan should include Internet and social networking elements. Such a strategy is advisable in the modern climate of e-commerce and smartphones. You and your communications advisors will benefit greatly from a long-term media outreach plan because it will teach you to be proactive in your use of media and to develop the professionalism that is necessary for effective communications to modern audiences.

If you don't have the luxury of an in-house team of experts to coach you – and most non-profit leaders don't – dozens, if not hundreds, of competent professionals are at your fingertips through the wonder of the Internet, able and willing to help you for a fee. Sometimes real experts are right in your own town and easily identifiable through a web search. Tap into their expertise: it will pay you back a hundred-fold.

I remember meeting Wendy Wright when she was the President of Concerned Women for America, a Christian conservative advocacy group based in Washington, DC. I have rarely been so impressed with a leader's public persona. It was not so much her track record of accomplishments (winning a Supreme Court case for free speech, testifying before Congress, advising international leaders, etc.) that impressed me, but what came across as her poise and utter *preparedness* for public life. She was able to speak to any audience, in any format, at any time about her mission's particular issues, and often went head to head with her ideological enemies in spirited debates. Furthermore, she always presented herself to others with a powerful sense of optimism and joy that radiated from her. We all need to be this type of leader: capable, positive, and energetic in the promotion of our mission.

In short, to be an effective promoter of your cause and mission, you must equip yourself to be conversant in most, if not all, forms of modern media and respond to any media invitation whenever possible. More than one effective communicator has converted a soul to a cause with words that touched a heart, but that can't be done unless you are "out there" and prepared to meet all the challenges of being a communicator *in the information age.*

6. *Money Follows Mission*

The most important fundraising principle for people of faith is this: money follows mission. This principle seems counterintuitive. We think that we can only do our mission if we first have the funds to operate. While "seed money" is necessary to begin any endeavor (we will address how to go about initiating funding in Chapter 5, Point 2, "Good Intentions"); in reality, the fundraising operates on the principle that money comes *as a result* of doing your mission effectively. Money follows mission, not the other way around.

It is human nature to want to support dynamic, inspiring, relevant, and effective efforts that show clear value or impact on the world. People donate to the individuals and groups that are doing *the things they would like to do* if they were not spending all their precious time raising kids, working jobs, and doing all the things their particular vocations demand of them.

An effective mission *earns* the support of good people who share your values. A dynamic mission inspires, it motivates, it solicits the heartfelt good will of people and their affection for a cause. In other words, good people in a philanthropic culture like ours will pay others to implement their deepest-held values when they can't do it themselves. There is absolutely nothing wrong with people living vicariously off the idealistic and heroic efforts of others. (We do it all the time when we pay to watch movies, sports, theatre, etc. so why not do it for God and a good cause?)

Speaking strictly from a Christian perspective and experience, the community of faith will always support your mission if it inspires them. You carry out the mission with a deep trust in God's Providence, and as long as you are a good steward of the resources He sends you, His blessings will sustain your mission through the generosity of believers who are predisposed to give to righteous causes. All of Jesus' parables about stewardship in the Gospel tell us that God rewards the responsible use of resources and provides for His missionaries (Matthew 25:14-30; Luke 16:1-15; Luke 19:12-28). This does not mean that fundraising is easy or automatic. All trust implies a certain amount of risk, a holy risk that is part of a Christian's worldview, and your mission is no exception to that rule.

St. John Bosco, the Founder of the Salesian order in the 19th Century, was famous for making big decisions to *spend money before he had it*, but that forced him onto his knees daily and into the position of beggar more times than he would have liked to admit. That is where leaders should be.

St. Maximilian Kolbe built the largest monastery in the world in the poverty of pre-World War II Poland and also an international publishing organization that extended as far as Japan, on the power of his phenomenal risk-taking, something to which he was not suited by temperament or training. He did it all with trust in the Virgin Mary's intercession for him and in the power of his faith that God would provide.

And then there is the famous story that Raymond Arroyo tells of Mother Angelica, Foundress of the massive EWTN media empire, who "purchased" a $600,000 satellite dish before she had the money to pay for it. When the truck showed up to install the dish and collect the money, she went into the chapel to beg Jesus for help – "Well, it's *your* satellite dish," she said to the Lord – only to find that her prayer was cut short by a wealthy donor calling from a boat in the Caribbean wanting to donate the exact amount of money she needed!

Money is not the determining factor for the success of a holy mission. Faith is. Having a dependency on faith, however, is a far cry from saying that a mission can operate *without* material resources or that raising money is effortless. Material resources are only the efficient cause of the mission and one of the many things that keeps the gears moving. God does not suspend the laws of nature and economics simply because someone has good intentions.

As the stories of holy risk-takers indicate, the *mission* always comes first, but is imbued with a *steadfast faith* in God's blessing as well as *concerted efforts* to cooperate with God's grace in obtaining the necessary support. All these factors have to be in place for there to be a successful mission.

Keep in mind that risk-taking also has a downside. The ebb and flow of finances can be torture. When fundraising wanes and there is not enough cash in the coffers to cover the bills; when income declines because of donor whims and fancies; when you have to go into debt to accomplish your goals or ask people to make sacrifices in order to get by for another day— these are the times that test the resolve of leaders to live on faith and trust that God really will provide for their needs. Holy risk-taking is not *rash decision-making*; it is the determination to put the mission first and to live as though God were really in charge of the world (because He is).

7. *Stay Constantly in Front of Them*

One of the hallmarks of a true leader is his steadfast determination to preach his message, as St. Paul says, "whether it is convenient or inconvenient" (2 Timothy 4:2). The Gospel message takes root in people's hearts through the minister's fidelity to his task of going out into the mission field and staying in front of people, no matter how limited his audience may be at any given time. God is the one who multiplies the seed for the sowing and grants increase to all evangelizing efforts (cf. 2 Corinthians 9:10). The leader's virtue is to be relentless in getting his message out. This was Jesus' missionary style. In His public ministry, He travelled little more than sixty miles from where He was raised, but His was not an effort at mass-marketing. His message caused a change of hearts because of His relentless determination to go about Galilee "doing good and healing all who were oppressed by the devil" (Acts 10:38).

Being in front of people as much as possible allows them to know you and your thought patterns. It allows you to establish your credentials as an authority on an issue and gives you a chance to build trust with an audience. The more you connect with people, the more you become a known quantity to them. Familiarity is helpful in promoting anything.

There is also a natural ripple-effect of being in front of others: the more they see and hear you, the more they themselves will spread the message, and the greater number of people will be exposed to what you have to say. It was that ripple-effect that caused the non-Jewish Greeks to seek Jesus out through the disciples (cf. John 12:21). The rumors of an itinerant preacher going to the people caused even the wicked Herod to be curious about Jesus (cf. Luke 9:7-9).

As a general spiritual principle, staying in front of people with a saving message makes it possible for them to be converted in heart and mind. The message bears no fruit when hidden under a bushel basket (cf. Matthew 5:15 and Luke 11:33). St. Paul says that "faith comes from hearing" and wonders aloud, "How can they believe in him of whom they have not heard?" (Romans 10:14-15).

As a leader of a social change apostolate, it is absolutely necessary for you to be out in the immense field of our cultural wasteland sharing the riches of your saving message with those who need to hear it. But keep in mind that education, service, and charity usually bear long-term fruits. Immediate results are not often the bottom line of a non-profit venture. How good it would be if we always got to reap the harvest and see the tangible effects of our work, but that is rare. St. Paul reminded the Corinthians that he "planted, Apollos watered, but God caused the growth. Therefore, neither the one who plants nor the one who waters is anything, but only God, who causes the growth" (1 Corinthians 3:6-7).

Staying in front of people has both a proactive and a reactive dimension to it. Leaders are proactive through mission planning and strategizing about how to have their greatest impact. (See Point 6, "Failing to Plan", in Chapter 4.) The reactive dimension of a mission is its ability to give quick, principled responses to any public matter related to the mission. Faith-based leaders frequently comment on cultural issues that exacerbate the social problems they are trying to solve. If you are convinced that the world needs to hear your message, you have to learn to be "opportunistic" in a good sense. It's not possible to respond to *every* triggering event in culture or politics, but there are always ample opportunities for leaders to speak out and highlight society's need for their particular cause.

One of the most effective organizations in the culture today is the Family Research Council, set up by Focus on the

Family in the '90s as its public policy arm in Washington, DC. Their President, Tony Perkins, is one of the most dynamic and consistent leaders you could ever meet. He is articulate, well-prepared in his answers, and up-to-date on all the public policy issues that affect Christian/family life in America. He and his team of excellent communicators model everything we have said so far about the effective promotion of a mission. They are relevant, consistent, timely, and proactive/reactive in their messaging without being reactionary, and they have the results to prove it. In 2018 they were in the forefront of bringing home an American pastor who was jailed in North Korea for many years. That was just one of their many advocacy victories and influential campaigns.

The ability to speak to people constantly, finding new ways to present the message, commenting on public issues, facing the media, preparing for talks, and overcoming your fears of criticism is not for the fainthearted. These leadership qualities require persistence, courage and zeal. You must pray for these spiritual gifts and human talents because God gives generously to those who ask. Then watch how God works to change the world through your message and mission.

8. *Don't Confuse Having an Audience with Having an Impact*

Good promotions are necessary for your mission as you attempt to change hearts and minds, but never confuse *having an audience with having an impact*. Promotion, by definition, presumes an audience. But audiences, with all their energy and enthusiasm, do not necessarily represent a *changed world*. They are already supporters, otherwise they would not be in your audience. Yes, some of your supporters will be true converts, already changed by your message, but most of your audience will consist of like-minded people who have no need to be converted. The untransformed world awaits you.

In fact, the feeling of commotion and movement, the act of stirring things up that comes with playing to an audience can be very seductive forces in the life of a leader: they can create the *illusion of significance* which nurtures pride and strokes a leader's ego. What you should really be concerned about in all your promotional efforts is the glory of God, the advancement of your worthy cause, prayer and the saving of souls. In deviating from those essential goals, you run the risk of being affected by all the negatives that come from fame and fortune.

There is a very personal aspect to this. To survive spiritually in the public eye for any length of time, you must learn to evaluate your personal popularity as a public figure differently than you evaluate your organization's impact. Having some positive effect on the larger world is always the result of the coordinated efforts of many people, a team, an organization rather than an individual. Furthermore, your organization's performance can often be measured against the objective standards and goals it sets for itself and is rarely the result of anyone's personal affection for the institution.

Personal popularity, however, is quite a different matter. It is the attachment of an audience to a public figure. Yet, while a leader may have many talents and accomplishments, his work as a representative of a mission is less that of a star performer than of a coordinator of the efforts and gifts of others. He may believe his *personal popularity is an indication that he himself is creating all the change* brought about by the mission and could easily lose sight of the communal impact his team or co-workers are creating. Sometimes personal popularity attracts admirers to a great mission, but the leader must not mistake his audience for personal impact or confuse it with the organization's impact.

The dangers of fame are very real. "Pride goeth before the fall" says the Book of Proverbs (cf. 16:18). Leaders are responsible for cultivating an honest self-assessment and a clear life of virtue at all times. Thomas à Kempis, in his 15th century classic, *The Imitation of Christ,* says, "The whole world cannot swell with pride the man who is subject to truth; nor will he be swayed by the flattery of all his admirers, if he has established all his trust in God."[4] Amen to that!

One of the best antidotes to pride is to always be loud *in praise of others*, regularly giving credit to other people for their contributions to the mission. Everyone loves to receive recognition, but you should never bestow it falsely. At best, people take it as flattery that does nothing to really motivate them to greater service. At worst, it leads to a kind of entitlement mentality where people expect to be praised and even rewarded for low performance.

A leader looks into the details of the machinery of his organization and *finds actual reasons* to praise the good work of others. There are always examples of unsung heroes on the front lines where few people go or of those silent warriors hidden in cubicles doing thankless but essential work. The leader who has his eyes open will see them and give the proper recognition that motivates his co-workers to keep performing well for the mission. More importantly, the leader who is paying attention to the contributions *of others* is less likely to be contemplating his own grandeur.

Finally, only a grateful heart remains humble. If you are imbued with a sense of divine purpose, it will be easy to see God's hand in all things. God Himself is the one who deserves the most credit but receives the least recognition! Thank Him, praise Him, glorify Him, and worship Him in all dimensions of your life and work, and you will never be seduced into thinking that *God needs you* to accomplish His works. It's exactly the other way around.

---

4   Thomas à Kempis, *Imitation of Christ*, Book III, Ch. 27.

Conclusion

A leader's promotion of his cause is a work that is never finished. The needs his mission addresses certainly never cease so the leader is never free from the duty of letting others know why and how his organization meets these particular problems and conquers them. The leader believes that changing the world happens one soul at a time through direct contact with people – staying in front of them – but he also believes that God provides many opportunities for effectively communicating a message. You are the leader, you incarnate the mission, you communicate it to others. Trust that God will provide both the resources needed to sustain the mission and the fruitfulness of it.

Chapter 3

Core Mission Principles

1. Think People Not Systems

2. Resist Mission Drift

3. Direct Engagement With the Enemy

4. Adapt or Die

5. Build a Performance Culture

6. Create a Culture of Joy and Celebration

7. Generous Stewardship of Limited Resources

8. The Mission Happens Outside the Building

> *A ship in harbor is safe – but that is*
> *not what ships are built for.*
>
> *~John A. Shedd*

1. Think People Not Systems

A leader knows that the only way to truly change the world is first to change hearts. Authentic societal change does not come primarily through systems, soul-less efficiency, power, money, or ideology. It comes through people. You, as a leader of a faith-based mission, have to think big about people and souls. You must be convinced that the Lord wishes to capture the hearts of every human being on the planet by means of *your* apostolate.

Prayer drives the mission, yes, but people implement and are the ultimate goal of the mission. A leader is constantly tempted to see his own programs, systems, and campaigns as the conduit of change. These are only means to an end, instruments in the hands of the human operators.

In his fascinating little book on leadership, *You Don't Need a Title to Be a Leader,* Mark Sanborn makes it clear that leadership is for those who

- lead through their relationships with others;

- collaborate rather than control;

- persuade rather than order people to contribute; and

- get others to follow them out of respect and commitment rather than fear and compliance.[1]

---

[1]   Mark Sanborn, *You Don't Need a Title to Be a Leader: How Anyone, Anywhere, Can Make a Positive Difference* (Colorado Springs: Waterbrook Press, 2006), xiv.

There is no single trait that fully defines an effective leader, but there are a number of traits that are essential. Being people-centered is one of those essentials.

This is why leaders of faith-based missions potentially have a greater positive effect on society than do political leaders. Politics uses coercive power to get things done and has almost no concern for the inner life of people or communities. Faith uses inspiration, motivation, and virtue to bring transformation. Recall the insight of Peter Drucker that managers do things right while leaders *do the right things*. We may add that a leader is also the one who inspires them to work with their whole hearts for the most important values that set people and societies free.

In an analogous way, a leader is both a shepherd and a parent to his associates. A leader knows his people and lets them get to know him. He learns their names, their spouses' and children's names. Without being intrusive, he regularly inquires about their interests, their history, their personal stories, what makes them tick. He thinks about them and their needs constantly.

Professionally, he sets them up for success and imagines ways they can be even more productive and personally fulfilled in their work. He finds creative ways to show them their value to the mission. Often, the associates know what kind of a difference they make for the mission because the leader tells them—and gives them opportunities to prove their mettle.

Maintaining a people perspective is the essence of leadership. The post-industrial, modern world invented the independent "organization" which organizes and channels human activity for efficiency; but every organization, the longer it exists, tends toward entropy, bureaucracy and abstraction. It runs the danger of becoming detached from the real concerns and needs of people.

In all humility, you must remember that the Lord does not need you or your ministry to accomplish the work of His

Kingdom. He came to establish a living Church, not a social service organization. He has many servants and does His best work in and through people. So does every good leader.

2. *Resist Mission Drift*

There are many tools[2] to help you avoid the deadly force of *mission drift*, defined as the incremental deviation of an organization from the essential purpose for which it was founded. Mission drift is usually a slow, often imperceptible, process. It is like the farmer in a field who fixes on a point in the distance to help him plow in a straight line, only to find out when he gets there that the fixed point was actually a slow-moving cow!

The real cause of mission drift is not normally the enemies *outside* the organization who try to knock you off course (though I will cite one example of this below) but the endless opportunities to get involved in the *other good projects* not strictly related to the mission. They are the slow-moving cows (not a personal metaphor about any individual, of course). Peter Drucker said in his book, *The Effective Executive*, that staying true to your mission "requires self-discipline and an iron determination to say 'No'"[3] (to other people's good ideas). Elsewhere, he stated plainly: "The word 'No!' is a complete sentence."

Steve Jobs, the founder of Apple Computers, echoed this same truth some years later:

> People think focus means saying "Yes" to the thing you've got to focus on. But that's not what it means at all. It means saying "No" to the hundred other good ideas that there are. You have to pick carefully. I'm actually as proud of the

---

2   See the "Web-Based Nonprofit Resources" at the end of this book for many valuable assets to help you take advantage of these tools.

3   Peter F. Drucker, *The Effective Executive* (New York: Harper and Row, 1967), 101.

things we *haven't* done as the things I have done. Innovation is saying "No" to a thousand things.[4]

One of the smallest words in the English language can pack a great punch when used to safeguard the integrity of your mission. This seems to be a favorite theme of great leaders, and it should be ours too.

Every single good idea and fabulous new opportunity that crosses a leader's desk must be held up to scrutiny and evaluated against the primary mission of the organization. It is not a good vs. evil struggle we are engaged in here. It is much harder. It's the contest between the good of *our mission* and a million other good things we could do.

The effective leader reinforces the primacy of his own mission every time he *vetoes* another great opportunity to get involved in someone else's project or even to indulge his own grand schemes that he should recognize – if he is honest with himself – as off-mission or low-priority. The iron discipline of saying "No" is first and foremost a very personal, interior discipline. Then it has two exterior dimensions, horizontal and vertical.

Horizontal Discipline

Horizontal discipline is the passionate desire to stay true to mission priorities *over time*. It is the ability to execute pre-set plans from start to finish without altering them in their essence. True victories, large or small, are won at the cost of many small sacrifices, sometimes over extended periods of time, that keep an initiative on course toward completion and according to plan.

Horizontal discipline is *about impact*. The leader asks: Are we doing A, B, and C because they feel good or because they

---

[4] Apple Worldwide Developers' Conference, 1997.

are true mission priorities? Have we altered the goals to fit other priorities that have come up in the meantime? Are we settling for quick results here? Have we lost sight of the overall goal? Do our words and actions *today* all line up with what we said we were going to do *yesterday* when we started this project? A disciplined leader keeps his mind on his own stated goals and makes sure he and his people stay on a straight path to accomplishing them.

Vertical Discipline

Vertical discipline is defined as the commitment to *a transcendent view* of the mission. For a secular organization this may not be anything more than holding to high legal and ethical standards, but for faith-based organizations, this has a spiritual dimension and is a life-giving discipline. Vertical discipline is seeking God's will in all things and a collective willingness to follow the guidance of His Spirit (cf. Luke 11:13).

This type of discipline differs from standard goal-setting and planning because it looks at results from a much wider perspective than worldly impact. Vertical discipline *asks questions about values and quality.* Is God pleased with this effort? Does it give Him glory? Are we settling for worldly victories and selling out for lesser results than our mission demands of us? Is A, B, or C a priority of yesterday's evangelization? Is this a publicity stunt or are we sincerely seeking new ways to evangelize? Is this initiative full of prayer? What souls will be saved or touched by our efforts? What lives will be improved by our holy mission?

And frankly, sometimes mission drift *is provoked* from the outside, which may involve you in a kind of existential war to protect the integrity of your mission. This may be better described as mission attack or mission derailment, but the need to defend the mission from alteration is the same, as we will see by this next example.

The Boy Scouts of America (BSA) gives us an idea of what happens when an organization loses these two types of discipline. Starting sometime in the '90s, our country's premier organization for boys fought legal battles to resist the militant homosexual movement attempting to infiltrate their organization. They fought each battle diligently for many years because the values of that ideology were totally alien to the BSA's core *mission* of forming young men to live lives of civic and godly character.

By 2015, however, the Boy Scouts were worn down by over a decade of anti-discrimination lawsuits and relentless social campaigns. They eventually caved in to the pressure. In that year, they allowed openly gay leaders into the movement, followed shortly thereafter by gay and transgender boys. In 2017 they decided to admit girls into their units and to drop the word "Boy" from their title, leaving them with the anemic (genderless) name of "Scouts" – and a devastated mission.

Unsurprisingly, by 2018 they had lost a third of their membership and were close to filing for bankruptcy.

Not every story of mission drift is as dramatic as what happened to the Boy Scouts. To repeat our main concern: a leader's discipline consists mainly in resisting everything that waters down or threatens the integrity of the mission. Leaders focus only on *the best ideas that are* consonant with their own missions and leave everything else for other organizations to do.

3. *Direct Engagement With the Enemy*

A common flaw of faith-based missionaries is the tendency to stay in a certain comfort zone of "the saved" (those who see eye-to-eye with us) and to avoid contact with "the enemy" (our ideological opponents). I'm not advocating that we actively *seek out* conflict with the latter, but I do think it is important at least to have contact with and periodically engage in dialogue, debates, and sparring with our mission's stated foes. They can do us a lot of good.

Direct engagement with the enemy is not for the faint of heart, but it is often proof of the authenticity of our mission and our convictions. Without it, we tend to be like the moth that flies frantically around a fire enjoying its warmth and light but never taking a risk of getting his wings singed by contact with the flames. Enemies often act like the "refiner's fire" that "purifies the sons of Levi" (Malachi 3:2, 3) when we engage them in meaningful ways. Our greatest mission impact, though, may lie in the hearts and souls of the very people who call themselves enemies.

Years ago I had two co-workers with an interesting history between them. One co-worker was a "convert" to our cause after having spent years in a movement that was totally antithetical to our own. She was an "enemy" in every sense of the word. But her dramatic change of values came when she heard a powerful presentation by one of our other associates that challenged her to the core. According to her own testimony, she *hated* him for it. "At that time, I considered So-and-So *my mor-tal e-ne-my!*" she would often emphatically say in talks. The truth he presented had shattered her proverbial comfort zone.

Yet, because that faithful associate was professional and untiring in taking the message to those who didn't agree with him, this woman heard the message more than once, and the power of the man's words and kindness eventually brought the "enemy" over to *our* side. It's my experience that most people who have ever been converted to a cause can name someone who cared enough to pray for them and speak the truth to them.

There are many stories of "enemies" who have been converted by persevering, attentive, non-hostile leaders who didn't hesitate to engage in a battle for their souls. The world-famous geneticist, Francis Collins, led the ground-breaking

Human Genome Project at a time when he identified himself as "an obnoxious atheist." Some generous soul gave him a copy of C.S. Lewis' *Mere Christianity*. After reading the first three pages Collins was intellectually honest enough to see that Lewis had obliterated his own childish arguments against faith. He soon converted to Christianity and became an apologist for the faith he used to persecute. We could cite many more stories of direct engagement with the enemy, but the point is clear.

Our friends, due to their natural affection for us, normally refrain from pointing out our weaknesses. Our enemies have no such scruples. They *always* find the chinks in our armor and sometimes exploit our weaknesses as a way to damage us and promote their own cause.

This leads to a final point: always remember that encounters with enemies are not usually festive occasions. They can lead to wounding, fatigue, and destruction. We cannot be naive when going toe-to-toe with foes. Jesus instructed us to be "wise as serpents and innocent as doves" (Matthew 10:16). He also sent His disciples out "two by two" for a reason. Never give in to the illusion that you are a lone white knight charging into battle against an enemy.

Direct engagement with the enemy helps mature us as missionaries of our cause, but it can't be our daily fare. Fraternal and spiritual support, preparation, training, wise counsel, regular decompression and rest time, post-mortem evaluations, etc. are all part of doing battle for the lives and souls of others. Enemies are important because they remind us of our need for God and the high stakes of the struggle for souls in this world.

4. *Adapt or Die*

Someone once said that to be human is to change, and to be fully human is to change often. That is true both for individuals and organizations. Every organization is like a living organism that needs to adapt to its environment in order to survive, but of course too much change and adaptation can also be harmful. Finding the elusive balance between change and stability is the job of a good leader. In our day, American culture is in a state of constant flux. Organizations that do not adapt to that rapid cultural change often wither and sometimes collapse. The famous American humorist, Will Rogers, said, "Even if you're on the right track, you'll get run over if you just sit there."[5] That's a wittier expression of this principle. Consider the following five items as realistic techniques for adapting to the modern cultural flux.

Creative Abandonment

Our oft-cited friend, Peter Drucker, coined the term "creative abandonment" in the mid-twentieth century to alert business leaders to their dangerous tendency to hold on to things that were not working. The dynamics are no different in the non-profit sphere. There should be no such thing as a "sacred cow" in an organization that exists to change the world. A leader should never be so attached to any one thing – even a very successful project – that he becomes overcommitted to it and unable to adapt to changing realities.

The reluctance to abandon or adapt projects once they cease to have any real effect on the outside world encumbers a mission. This is especially true with righteous causes. I have found that the greater the nobility of a cause, the more people tend to be attached to their own ideas about it. That is not a bad thing in an absolute sense unless the attachment turns into misguided zeal. Noble causes can end up driving organizations into the ground because their advocates often refuse to countenance any

---

[5]   Cited in Gary Keller and Jay Papasan, *The ONE Thing: The Surprisingly Simple Truth Behind Extraordinary Results* (Austin: Bard Press, 2012), 132.

adaptation or give an inch to innovation. And of course the soft, spiritual justifications for such a cause are, shall we say, legion.

Every project and program must be evaluated *according to its effectiveness for the mission*, using both quantitative and qualitative criteria to make an overall judgment.

Quantitative and Qualitative Analysis

Leaders don't do nostalgia, drama or entitlement. They do regular, hard-biting performance analysis to see if they and their people are living up to their core values.

Money is the easiest factor to evaluate since it can be quantified. Cost-effectiveness decisions must be made on the basis of the organization's mission priorities and the amount of funds available to implement them. Many programs, desirable in themselves, cannot be sustained, given the realities of cash flow. While we certainly operate with deep faith and sometimes take financial risks for our priorities, fiscal asceticism requires a regular no-nonsense evaluation of our uses of donor funds.

In the early part of my tenure at an international non-profit, it became clear that we could not sustain the cost of maintaining fixed offices in several different countries. These were holdovers from past administrations and, apparently, they worked well when they were set up. The world, however, had shifted underneath our feet by the time I got there. Even the boundaries of some countries had changed in the intervening period.

Above all, the offices had ceased to be effective ways to implement our mission. They were inefficient in their use of resources and poorly responsive to mission priorities. Other missionaries without offices in adjacent countries were accomplishing many more mission objectives with fewer resources. We also asked ourselves a very honest question that was relevant to our mission: In what sense is a *fixed office* "missionary"?

We decided that it wasn't, so we abandoned the fixed offices with all their costs and designated our most effective leaders to work from their homes as *coordinators* of the missionary work and personnel in their respective regions. The decision was, naturally, disappointing for some in our network who lost resources and offices, but it was a necessary adaptation to changing circumstances, and it was certainly for the good of the mission. More to the point, it transformed the missionary mindset and effectiveness of our missionaries.

Assessing *impact* is a qualitative exercise and more difficult for non-profits. Money can be counted; but impact has to be evaluated (note the root of this word: value). The spiritual works of mercy are intangible and therefore hard to quantify. The number of meals we feed the homeless is evident, but how do you measure compassion, inner transformation, insight or hope?

In the qualitative assessment we rely on the Gospel principle that "every tree is known by its own fruits" (Luke 6:44). The key evaluation question is *not*, "Is this a good and noble project?" (an abstract, subjective criterion) but rather, "Is this program *creating the change* that our mission requires?" (a specific, value-oriented criterion).

Instead of quantity questions, we can ask a whole host of related value questions: What is the specific evidence of change? Who has testified to the impact of our programs? How is this person, this family, this community, etc. *better* because of our work? Etc. Thus, mission change can be measured in a qualitative sense according to the mission's own values and the Gospel standard of spiritual "fruitfulness".

Fill In the Gaps

Following from the point about analysis, leaders in any change movement must look carefully for the "gaps" to fill (often called, "unmet needs") in their own movements to assess how their organization can make the biggest difference in their particular field of interest. This evaluation requires discernment, prayer, wisdom, and prudence because it is impossible to fill even a fraction of the needs in any area of human need. At the same time, organizations with similar missionary interests should strive to avoid needless duplication of efforts and destructive competition for donors. There are usually enough needs and supporters to go around!

Even if there are critical needs to be filled, leaders must not overextend their resources or capabilities either. They must humbly admit that there are things they cannot do and areas where they *cannot* have an impact. For years, one of the non-profit organizations I worked for toyed with the idea of setting up a research facility which, in the initial assessment, would have supported the other projects of our mission. There was a great need for it at the time, but we ultimately judged that we could not do it because it would have required too great an institutional commitment of time and funds. We also lacked the expertise to do it well, so we simply re-dedicated ourselves to our fundamental mission objectives.

The essential truth is that mission effectiveness requires leaders to make judgments as to how their limited resources can have the greatest impact on the actual needs of people. If you want to change the world, you must first discern where the need for change is greatest – and then boldly go there to fill it.

Change Just When Things Are Going Well

It is counterintuitive to change something just when things are going well, but it is a healthy practice and a very good principle of adaptation. The idea behind this principle is simple: programs usually conform to the cycles of birth, growth, peak and decline that are inherent in every living thing in the natural world. Even the most successful organizations don't experience continuous success.

We have all seen actors or athletes who have stayed on the scene long after their prime, still longing for their glory days, and it seems like everyone but the aging performer recognizes that fact. Peter Drucker lays out the logic of this "change at the peak" mentality well:

> Refocus and change the organization *when you are successful.* When everything is going beautifully. When everybody says, "Don't rock the boat. If it ain't broke, don't fix it." At that point, let's hope, you have some character in the organization who is willing to be unpopular by saying, "Let's *improve* it." If you don't improve it, you go downhill pretty fast. The great majority of major institutions that have gotten into real trouble...are successes that rested on their laurels.[6]

There are also leaders who rest on their laurels. King David's unfortunate tryst with Bathsheba came "after the king had taken up residence in his house and the Lord had given him rest from all his enemies on every side" (2 Samuel 7:1). In other words, when David was most "successful", he got lazy! That's when leaders and organizations get into trouble. Sloth and boredom are also standard human failings and more typical than most people would like to admit.

An organization is often wise to begin adapting a program just when it reaches the peak of its success. This attitude helps an organization stay hungry for improvement and avoid dependence on any program as a be-all and end-all of the mission. It takes courage to admit that a certain pet project does not have eternal value for the organization (those with noble causes often believe otherwise). Adapting and changing *successful* programs is part of the discipline of keeping your

---

[6]   Drucker, *Non-Profit*, 66-67.

mission focus, but, as Drucker notes, the change is actually the improvement, not the abandonment, of something that is working.

No one said this would be easy to do. A leader who wants to change X, Y, or Z when all is going well runs up against naysayers, vested interests, and a few who will call him crazy. Some fear for their jobs, and these real fears should not be easily dismissed. The leader who has to make hard decisions should communicate effectively with his co-workers during times of transition, treat people fairly, and in every way focus his team back on the mission and its rationale. Change is not easy, but change can bring innovations and opportunities to do your mission more effectively.

Stay Uncomfortable

Finally, a key adaptation principle is to always "stay uncomfortable" with the status quo. Never allow yourself or your people to settle into complacency, as King David did. This does not mean you have to create a high stress work environment or force everyone to perform to their maximum capacity every day. These are just as destructive to morale as complacency. Staying uncomfortable means that the organization as a whole is like Drucker's non-conformist who maintains a *dissatisfaction with mediocrity* and has a burning desire to improve on the status quo. This attitude needs to become part of the whole organization's work ethic.

The military calls this attitude "readiness". In the non-profit world, the readiness ethic translates into doing your mission and all its tasks with a high degree of zeal, professionalism and even a bit of edginess – a kind of productive unrest where one is never satisfied until he has gone the extra mile for the mission. Leaders and their organizations should always be uncomfortable; they change and adapt often and stay at the top of their games to maintain a strong mission.

5. *Build a Performance Culture*

As we've said, non-profit organizations exist to change the world through changed hearts. That's as it should be. American ingenuity has perfected the concept of the charitable organization, which exists for this high purpose and not for commerce as such. While non-profits are motivated by the highest ideals, they often have some unique performance hindrances that businesses don't have. Here are a few:

- Non-profits don't have the pressures of competition for market share to *push* them to higher standards of achievement;

- They are not driven by the "bottom line" of making money or satisfying the economic demands of shareholders;

- Non-profits don't pursue prestige, power, or money but rather are dedicated to service.

For these and other reasons, the *pressure to produce*, common in commercial ventures, is not always driving non-profits, so they can often be soft on the can-do attitudes that businesses need in order to survive. Leaders of non-profits, therefore, must sometimes make extra efforts to create and foster a performance culture inside the organization. In light of these concerns, let us consider five ways leaders can produce and strengthen a performance culture:

Performance Standards

We noted above that value results are not easily measurable. *Performance* is. A performance culture is usually the fruit of clear *performance expectations that are* established from the very beginning of the hiring process, ratified by goal-setting, and reaffirmed through evaluations of one sort or another. Many volumes have been written on each of these issues, so leaders don't have to reinvent the wheel when it comes to these standard practices.[7]

One common weakness of non-profit leaders is that they praise performance standards but neglect to impose penalties for lack of performance when their associates don't measure up to them. (This means they don't *fire* people when they should.) This is a leadership weakness that negatively affects the overall performance, and sometimes the morale, of an organization if bad apples remain on staff for too long.

All the effective leaders I know maintain a three-strikes-and-you're-out policy that balances reasonable indulgence of human failure with a priority on performance. A leader should not rule by fear or by holding jobs over people's heads, yet he should uphold high standards with reasonable expectations of performance. The organization cannot accomplish its mission effectively without them.

Hire and Keep Actual Performers

It goes without saying that a performance culture is built by having *real performers* on staff. Every leader must embrace the important duty of evaluating, removing, replacing, or re-assigning associates to areas of greater effectiveness. This is a difficult task for anyone with a heart, but it is also the burden of leadership.

When I came into a floundering non-profit some years ago, one employee immediately requested a meeting with me and used a good portion of the meeting to assure me, oddly, that "So-and-So is really good people." In fact, he boosted three of his favorite co-workers in the organization in an obvious

---

[7] Study the resources available at the back of this book for insight into creating a performance culture.

attempt to color my view of them prior to my initial staff evaluation process. Each one of them was "good people" all right, but I discovered that two of the three were totally incompetent and had to be let go – as did the "good people" promoter himself. That incident revealed several obvious reasons why the organization was floundering.

A leader's first responsibility is to safeguard the *integrity of the mission*, and this often means making difficult personnel decisions. In the aftermath of 9/11 in 2001, many non-profits took a hit on fundraising, as did the one I was serving, which made it necessary for me to lay off a certain percentage of my staff. This was a real heartbreaker. I met personally with each person chosen for the layoff, gave them generous severance payments according to their seniority, and thanked them genuinely for their service.

I did not apologize for those decisions, though, because keeping the organization alive was my personal responsibility as leader and also because layoffs are not a moral failing for which a leader has to apologize. Still, from a human standpoint, there is hardly a more difficult task a leader must face.

However, I also shared the sacrifice with those who were affected. I took a pay cut of my own meager wage. I lost several days of sleep and agonized over all the decisions. I also communicated clearly and honestly with the rest of the staff to calm further fears and orient them to the future.

In the grand scheme of things, the layoffs were the critical factor in the survival and long-term growth of the mission. "Downsizing" affects everyone, but it usually injects realism and often vibrancy into an organization.

No Rewards for Good Intentions

Good intentions do not make a good performer. Only *actual performance* makes a good performer. Leaders of non-profit organizations or ministries have to emphasize this principle often because altruistic people often believe that good intentions *are the mission.*

Spiritually-oriented people can sometimes have an insidious sense of entitlement for their cause. In its worst expression, they believe that *a vague someone* (usually their church or society in general) *owes* them funding for their noble projects, or they believe that their projects will just fall into place without much effort. We all wish things worked that way, but they don't. Leaders cast this entitlement demon out of their own hearts first and then root it out of their organizations.

The first challenge comes in the hiring process. True performance organizations hire only those people who have *track records of performance in the skill-sets and capacities the organization needs,* not a track record of failures, mediocre performance, or high aspirations for performance.

Hiring well-intentioned *non-performers* can be catastrophic for an organization, but it usually just mires the mission in mediocrity. You only need to be burned once to realize how painful – and costly – a hiring mistake can be. There is no infallible guarantee that even a person with a strong resume and good interviews will turn out to be a good performer in *your* organization; nevertheless, there is no excuse for hiring people with no realistic expectation that they will perform well.

Hire only those people who have good track records, good references, and good enthusiasm – not good intentions. There are many excellent resources that teach leaders the art of hiring for performance.[8] Study them and learn to hire well.

---

[8]   Start with a great short article by Curtis Chang, "Three Nonprofit Hiring Mistakes to Avoid," *Stanford Social Innovation Review,* 9/29/2011, easily found on the web. Then see the "Web-Based Nonprofit Resources" in the Helpful Resource section at the back of this book.

Avoid Family Hiring[9]

I've found that hiring immediate family members of current employees is bad policy because it often handicaps performance in an organization. That is not a universal opinion among managers and leaders, but it is mine. Every leader must develop a coherent policy in this regard. In my experience, direct family relationships make it hard for leaders to remain objective in their judgments about performance because, when push comes to shove, most people feel obliged to favor relatives in decision-making or cut them some slack in difficult situations, and that can negatively affect the internal culture of an organization.

Family members can hamstring disciplinary decisions too. A leader who gets one staff member mad at him for a disciplinary action inevitably gets *several* people mad at him if the staff member has family working in the same organization.

Larger organizations can get away with hiring family members on a policy of no direct reporting to a relative, but even then, family relationships invite potential tensions between staff members, as well as the danger of nepotism. The leadership of an organization should have a clear policy on this matter that favors the right of management to be unencumbered by potential family conflicts.

Recognition

Finally, good performance ought to be *publicly recognized,* and superior performance should be *rewarded* on a regular basis. Many leaders are deficient in the important skill of affirming their associates for great performance. Sometimes that is due to their own histories of meager or no encouragement. Many bosses believe that promotions, raises or perks are sufficient

---

9   This section does not address family-owned businesses and ministries, which have dynamics all their own and are beyond the scope of our treatment here.

recognition for good employees, but, in fact, a plethora of modern surveys indicates that appreciation and recognition are more important in producing job satisfaction than financial benefits alone.

I once worked in a warehouse with hundreds of employees where the managers had a strong ethic of employee affirmation. In their five- to seven-minute staff huddles before each shift began, the bosses highlighted the efforts of team members who went above and beyond the call of duty or those who performed with particular excellence. I recall my surprise at hearing them describing a few of the accomplishments of one of my unassuming team members whose talents I had seriously underestimated in the daily shuffle of work! Each story of superior performance made everyone appreciate everyone else a little more and provided the motivation for greater performance in our own tasks.

Learn the leadership art of affirmation, motivation, and encouragement. Gestures of appreciation, even if *seemingly* small, act like oil that lubricates the gears of a working machine. Leaders who reward, recognize, and encourage strong performance usually get more of it.

6. *Create a Culture of Joy and Celebration*

Nothing more symbolizes a vibrant mission than a sense of joy in the workforce. How dreary and serious some missionaries are! All teams get bogged down in negativity at times; in fact, this is especially true for those who fight for humanitarian causes. But a leader who understands the debilitating power of the problems his people face everyday looks for opportunities to create joy and celebration. These are a *spiritual antidote* to the negativity of mission stress. Joy raises people's souls to loftier ideals and reminds them that life is full of goodness, not just drudgery and pain. There are many ways to keep that positive spirit alive in an organization.

A leader cultivates an environment of joy around him by first having his own sense of humor, especially in times of adversity. The famed writer, Norman Cousins, once came down with a painful immune system disease and was given the bad news that his condition was terminal. To complement some minimal treatments by his doctor, Cousins decided that "laughter was the best medicine". His self-administered daily therapy consisted of heavy doses of vitamin C, Marx Brothers films and some old Candid Camera clips. By his own account, Cousins cured his immune system primarily by *laughing* for a period of time every day.[10] It's an amazing and true story, but I'm sure the doctor wouldn't prescribe this cure for everyone!

Another concrete measure is for the leader to periodically set aside the stress and problems of the mission to get outside the workplace with his associates. Natural occasions like birthdays, anniversaries, organizational milestones, great performances, even visits from outsiders can be wonderful opportunities to celebrate people and their goodness. The joy that comes with celebration is a reinforcement of our spiritual conviction that *life definitively conquers death*, both now and in eternity. Christian missions should be tangible expressions of a Resurrection mentality if nothing else.

As a general rule, when well-balanced joy and celebration reign in a group of people with a mission, it overflows into the hearts of all who come into contact with them.

7. *Generous Stewardship of Limited Resources*

Anyone who works for a charitable organization is certainly not doing it for the money. If you have worked for any length of time in business, you understand the difference between the two worlds of work and even of the difference in basic motivations

---

[10]   Phil Taylor, *Set Yourself On Fire! How to Ignite Your Passions and Live the Life You Love!* (Mechanicsburg, PA: Tremendous Life Books, 2010), 82-32.

for working. Most people work to live. Missionaries live to work – for a cause in which they deeply believe.

I once had an employee who came to our organization from an up-and-coming tech firm. He accepted a significantly lower salary to join our team but told me that the "value differential" (his term) of a non-profit was more important to him than his previous higher salary. In his estimation, the many intangible aspects of the work compensated for the drop in income. For one thing, our regular work hours were more humane than in his tech job, and his kids were glad to have their dad back.

This employee had a good sense of his family's needs and resources and brought that healthy spirit into our organization. This attitude is what we call stewardship. There is a vague concept of stewardship as "tithing" – which it is, in a strict, biblical sense – but it is more. In non-profit work, stewardship is an honest perception of the totality of one's limited resources and the creativity to use them in a way that is most effective and pleasing to God.

Charitable organizations depend on the voluntary contributions of hardworking people to sustain their mission. They exist on the "widow's mite" (Mark 12:41-44), and they should never forget that. Good stewardship puts the sacrificial donations of supporters to responsible use in everything from salaries and travel, to programs and projects, to the purchase of equipment and material assets for the mission.

When one of the non-profits I worked at needed reliable transportation, a more experienced manager told me that we should never purchase a *new* vehicle for our organization because a used vehicle with low mileage and a good maintenance record was of equal or better value and significantly lower in cost. *"It's better stewardship"*, he said. That was both a personal and an organizational learning lesson for me.

The non-profit organization should be equitable in salary and benefits to its employees with the understanding that

Gospel values promise a "living wage" but not necessarily a comfortable lifestyle! Non-profits generally don't sell products or sustain their operations through investments, so the remuneration packages of a non-profit can never be expected to parallel those of the business world.

At the same time, there are many ways a leader can be generous to his people without having to dole our money or increase salaries. He may give time off, performance recognition, travel and training opportunities; he may assure that his associates always have sufficient resources and stable financial backing for their projects, etc.

Of course, the spiritual and community assets of a mission are often the greatest benefits for everyone involved. These intangibles are part of the overall "compensation package" in a very real sense, even though they do not show up on balance sheets.

The stewardship-minded leader asks hard questions: I know what I'd like to do, but does this expenditure fit our mission objectives? Will this investment of time, talent, treasure advance an essential work of ours? Is the expense actually necessary or can we do this another way without incurring the expense?

None of these questions is about the *quantity* of money or resources expended. They all have to do with the attitude of people toward using the organization's limited resources to carry out its mission as well as the value of the expected outcome.

Frugality doesn't exclude spending money, sometimes a great deal of it, for priorities or long-term investments that may not have a lot to show in the short-run. Staff training, equipment upgrades, capital investments and the like fall into this category. But any long-term investment of resources must be reviewed periodically to assure that the expenditure was responsible and effective. It cannot be forgotten in the day-to-day workings of the organization or passed off with an "Oh well, that didn't work" attitude when it fails. Faith-based organizations don't have the luxury of government officials who spend other peopl*e's* money with no accountability for results.

Non-profit leaders are accountable not only to their generous donors, but also to God for their stewardship of His blessings. The parables of the Dishonest Steward (Luke 16:1-8) and of the Talents (Matthew 25:14-30) make it clear that stewardship of resources is a serious value of God's Kingdom.

Above all, a leader must be honest and upfront about his organization's financial reality and train his people to be generous stewards. The leader is like a father of a family who teaches his maturing kids incremental lessons about how to handle money. His duty is not only to dole out cash for their legitimate needs but also to teach them the *value* of money and the need for fiscal responsibility in all things. The goal is to develop an organization-wide sense of stewardship of their limited resources. (We'll have more to say about "fiscal realism" in Chapter 5, sections 1 and 2.)

8. *The Mission Happens Outside the Building*

The final mission principle is one that should be self-evident but is often entirely overlooked by staffers; namely, that the frontlines mission, the organization's point of impact, takes place *outside* the building. The office exists for the mission and not the other way around. Peter Drucker would say that all the opportunities are outside the building, while all the *costs* are inside. Inside workers need to feel a sense of ownership of the tangible mission that takes place in the field, but creating that connectedness for them is a leadership challenge.

Staff members who don't have first-hand experience of the outside mission are at a disadvantage in comprehending its full scope. That is understandable. They're not on the front lines; they cannot "see" how their work fits into the overall mission even though they may have a sincere zeal for the cause. The opposite is also true: people on the front lines need to be made aware of the silent and sometimes heroic generosity of the support staff. Furthermore, each part of the organization may be unaware of what the other parts are doing.

The best way to foster that greater awareness of the mission among the associates, therefore, is to keep everyone focused on the problems "out there", even if their jobs never require them to leave the building. Images are the best way to make this translation for both the inside and outside missionaries. As mentioned in Chapter 2, you must paint living pictures of the mission for your people. Learn to use graphics, images, stories, testimonies and even living witnesses to creatively portray the mission for all who can't be on the front lines. The only limit to making presentations of this sort is in the creativity of the leader. A good leader reminds everyone in the mission of why they work and for whom they work.

Perhaps the most effective way to foster mission realism among your associates is to have office workers periodically accompany the mission staff on a trip, even if it is something as simple as attending a local event with them. Drucker says that a leader sometimes has to

> ...force your people, and especially your executives, to be on the outside often enough to know what the institution exists for. There are no results inside an institution. There are only costs. Yet it is easy to become absorbed in the inside and to become insulated from reality. Effective non-profits make sure that your people get out in the field and actually work there again and again.[11]

Again, the converse is also true: asking outside associates to visit the main place of operations is crucial to making the mission come alive for all stakeholders. The costs of such travel are not inconsequential, but they are an investment in the task

---

[11] Drucker, *Effective Executive*, 120.

of molding all aspects of an organization into a coherent whole. It is money well-spent.

This is particularly important in a large organization with many more loosely-related affiliates. How delighted I always felt when my in-house associates would meet one of our visiting affiliates and hear them say, "Oh, you're So-and-So! I've been communicating with you all this time, and now I'm finally meeting you!" That moment of awakening, connectedness, and joy is one of the most blessed results of bringing people together from different fields of the same mission and letting the Holy Spirit unite them and inspire them to greater generosity and zeal.

Reminding your people that the mission takes place outside the building creates cohesion: your teams become truly apostolic, your organization as a whole pulls together and operates with greater unanimity of mind and heart, and your associates' view of the mission will never be abstract or unrealistic. They will also be less likely to indulge in pettiness and short-term thinking because they will understand themselves as missionaries, even though they might only be doing the thankless job of pushing paper. The long-term fruit of this cultivation is a strong sense of "job satisfaction" and even excitement that the team feels in playing an essential part in a life-changing mission.

Conclusion

A missionary spirit is the essence of every faith-based organization. This spirit generates support, inspires commitment, and unifies the many talents and energies of the faithful. The non-profit leader is the visible representative of that mission to the world and the one responsible not just for the basic survival of the organization but also for its strength, dynamism and productiveness.

You, as leader, must never lose sight of the need for God's grace that makes a mission flourish. That is the foundation of all missionary endeavors. But you must also remember that tried-and-true people skills and principles of operation are the bread and butter of a leader's expertise.

Chapter 4

Core Organizational Principles

1. Your People Want You to Be In Charge

2. First Things First

3. Find the Inside/Outside Balance

4. Regular Staff Training

5. Flow Chart Discipline

6. Failing to Plan is Planning to Fail

7. Hire For Work Ethic and Productivity

8. Manage Your Board

There are two ways to do something:
the right way, and again.

~Navy SEALs

1. *Your People Want You to Be In Charge*

The expectation of a leader is simple but daunting: that he be in charge of his sphere of authority – constantly. He is the organizational point man. The buck stops with him. His people want him to be the resolute holder of the office, and they expect him to exercise that authority forthrightly and courageously.

People do not want an autocrat, a narcissist or an arrogant person to lead them of course, but they always want a *strong* leader. Such a leader embodies the strength of the mission and organization, makes them proud of their work, and in turn strengthens them in their own commitments and work ethic. They will follow a strong leader, even if they disagree with him or personally dislike him, but not if they think he is dishonest. Honesty and integrity are part of a principled leadership style; vice, moral compromise, and corruption have no place in it.

Poor leadership may put the wellbeing of whole communities at stake. Compare the heroic churchmen in Eastern Europe who stood against Communism in the 20th century with the church leaders who became Communist puppets. There you will see the overarching value of strong leadership.

The faith communities whose leaders sold out to Communist governments either completely disappeared or became shadows of themselves over time. In contrast, the churchmen who stood strong against the atheistic system often went to jail and endured torture, but their communities "kept the faith" in solidarity with them, even if those communities were deprived of sacramental ministers or had to worship clandestinely.

There is no better example of this than the faithful Christians in Ukraine where the population was decimated by Josef Stalin's genocide in the early '30s, the infamous Holodomyr. Throughout Stalin's entire evil regime, non-cooperating Orthodox, Catholic and Protestant churches alike were driven underground. When Communism disappeared as a political system after 1991, those same faithful churches emerged after six decades in exile and re-established themselves very quickly and vibrantly. Most of their leaders had spent years, even decades in jail, but the faithful recognized them as *real leaders*. By their heroic refusal to renounce or even compromise their faith, those leaders' were more present to their people from jail than if they had been with them in person.

Non-profit leadership in the 21st century presents us with many opportunities for heroism, though perhaps not as dramatic as those who suffered under Communism. Most Christian leaders in the West[1] probably won't go to jail for their beliefs, but they may find themselves hauled into court. I vividly remember the systematic judicial persecution of the heroic men and women of Operation Rescue in the '90s. I knew some of them and was horrified by the injustices these good people endured as the persecutions of the Clinton Administration transpired. These heroes were constantly in and out of jails and courts for their righteous witness against the evils of abortion.

The day-to-day running of non-profit missions is more prosaic. A faith-based leader expresses strong leadership through his professional competence and attitude of service. He may have the last word on any given decision, but he makes sure his decisions are based on sound advice and research. He leads meetings, he supervises, he delegates work to those associates

---

[1] The horrible reality of Christian persecution worldwide is a larger story that I cannot address here. The non-profit called Open Doors USA is a phenomenal resource for understanding the larger problem. It is easily found on the Web, www.opendoorsusa.org.

tasked with getting the job done. He knows what's going on in every department and in every dimension of the mission. He is in touch with the inner workings of his team(s) as well as in charge of the overall functioning of the organization. He always wants to know, and he *should* know all that goes on in the organization. It's his responsibility to be on top of things.

Your strong leadership doesn't mean that you micromanage everything; it means that you exercise authority well and keep your finger on the pulse of the living, breathing mission of the organization and its missionaries. That's what people want of you – to be in charge – and ultimately what they need for their own effectiveness in carrying out the mission. And if someday you are "persecuted for the sake of righteousness" (Matthew 5:10) like many strong leaders before you, blessed will you be!

2. *First Things First*

As a basic organizing principle,[2] the leader has to decide which of the many objectives of the mission need to be prioritized. He must keep those priorities at the forefront of his thinking about the mission at all times. We generally do that in our personal lives too. I recall a lady in a church I once belonged to who wrote all of her "to do" items on a simple yellow pad every morning and got an enormous amount of productive work done every day. It was the simplest of organizing systems but she would have qualified for an executive position in any decent-sized organization despite never having gone to college. She kept her priorities displayed in black and yellow before her eyes every day. You don't need the perfect day planner to keep your priorities in the right order, you only need to pay careful attention to first things first.

---

[2]   Taken from the title of Chapter 5 of Peter Drucker's 1985 masterpiece, *The Effective Executive.*

The mission statement is the starting point for determining what goes first. Like my friend with the yellow pad, keeping clear about priorities is more effective if they are written down and on display around the workspaces. Graphic reminders of the top organizational priorities of the mission create a focused work environment.

Jeff Bezos, founder of Amazon, keeps his company's mission statement plastered on the walls of every Amazon fulfillment center. Here it is in all its simplicity: "To be Earth's most customer-centric company". That's what drives the mega-monster enterprise of Amazon. It's a fantastic mission statement. Each time Bezos' employees walk by one of those signs, carefully positioned at eye-level, they get reminded of their reason for working. There is no such thing as too much repetition, verbal and visual, of your mission.

A commitment to keeping mission priorities in the forefront means that you refuse to live by the seat of your pants. Disruptions, dysfunctions and crises are part of any organization's life, but you can't let crisis management be your normal way of operating. These things are only the normal mission of hospital emergency rooms!

"First things first" is a discipline and a mindset. The common human tendency is to take the path of least resistance or to do easier, low-priority items to make ourselves feel that we are accomplishing something. A "second things first" attitude weakens a mission work ethic if the leader allows it to become endemic in the organization.

Peter Drucker's phrase, "an iron determination to say 'No'" describes a leader's attitude toward safeguarding his mission priorities. It's a habit most human beings don't come by naturally. We all want to say "Yes" to other people's needs and projects. Drucker recommends time tracking[3] as an aid to

---

[3]   See Chapter 2 of *The Effective Executive*, "Know Thy Time."

developing this hard discipline. Keep a daily log, jotting down exactly how you spend your time, and after a couple weeks of this, evaluate whether or not you are spending your time working on *actual* priorities. This practice is an eye-opener for most leaders.

The good of the mission is the first organizational priority of any leader. Keep first things first – and let the other chips fall where they may.

3. Find the Inside/Outside Balance

We have said elsewhere that the mission happens outside the building (Chapter 3, Point 8). True. As the public face of the organization, the leader must be "out there" doing his mission, but he must also have an intimate knowledge of and contact with the inner workings of his organization. That means he has to manage a dual responsibility: he must find the proper inside/outside balance.

The familiar image of the scales of justice may provide a good example of this delicate balance: Lady Justice wears a blindfold and holds a scale with two hanging trays. With nothing weighing them down, the trays naturally reach equilibrium and balance out perfectly. When you add something of weight to one tray, the equilibrium is temporarily upset. You then add an item of equal weight to the other tray to return balance to the scales.

The same holds true for our duties, which can easily be imagined as weights (i.e., burdens). The things we have to do inside the organization rest on one tray and our responsibilities in the mission field rest on the other. Lady Justice's blindfold indicates that this inside/outside balance *is more a matter of feel* than of measuring. In other words, the best leaders *intuit* the balance of the two trays rather than falsely trying to *impose* balance on them through precise formulas or time management schemes.

A non-profit leader has many responsibilities: fundraising, media, donor relations, travel and speaking engagements, networking, writing for publications and reports, board meetings, community events, overseeing major projects and initiatives, supervising direct reports, etc. Some responsibilities fit easily into one of the two categories, but others are divided between inner and outer (fundraising, for example, requires a lot of internal focus and management but is essentially a matter of public relations for the leader). It is the leader's job to look at all his areas of responsibility and assign them to one side or the other of his scales of justice on any given day.

The "blind" holder of the scales learns balance through trial and error. He gets a feel for how far the scales tip to the right or to the left only by doing his mission and making mistakes in scheduling and prioritization. He shouldn't fear making mistakes (as if he could avoid them!) Like a child who learns to ride a bike by falling to one side or the other, mistakes and falls are our best teachers of balance, as long as we don't have a serious accident. Eventually, the blindfolded holder of the scale develops a *feel* for the balance point of his responsibilities and returns the scales back to center when they tip too far to one side or the other.

Travel for job-related concerns is a particularly difficult balancing act to get right. Long periods of time out of the office are sometimes unavoidable, but they are rarely healthy. A leader needs time with his associates for the sake of their morale, their motivation, their professional development. Like skipping a son's or daughter's special event, there is an emotional downside to a leader's absence.

I recall having one position that required inordinate amounts of travel, or at least I thought so when I first came on. In the early stage of my tenure I took a very long trip (I believe it was nearly two weeks) that I judged was necessary to address a festering problem somewhere in our network. Well, I judged wrongly. Two weeks was entirely too much time to be away from my main base of operations in the early days of a new job, and I returned to what felt like a lifeless, demoralized group of co-workers. My travel responsibilities never ceased after that, but *I* had changed. Thankfully, I learned to balance my outside work better with everything else I had to do at the home base – and I began taking shorter trips!

A leader, especially a CEO, can almost never maintain that delicate inside/outside balance without a competent number two person watching over the regular operations. A leader simply cannot supervise the complex workings of a large organization by himself, nor should he try. The number two has to have the leader's trust, proper authorizations, and the necessary skills to keep the institution running while the boss is away. He needs management experience along with strong people skills because he has to maintain good morale and coordination among the staff to complement the boss's leadership.

Choosing the correct number two requires prayer, a careful search and clear discernment about who God wants to fill this position. Number two support is necessary for you and your team's productivity. No pilot flies without a co-pilot, and you shouldn't either. The best number two man I ever had often said to me: "It is *my* job to make *your* work for the mission more effective." He was worth his weight in gold.

4. *Regular Staff Training*

In the 1960s Peter Drucker coined the term "knowledge worker" to describe the typical professional in a modern organization, whether business or non-profit. The term pays tribute to the increasing technological sophistication of our society and global economy and describes the reality of what organizations need in great abundance: expertise. Whatever the field, the challenges of our complex modern world are immense and require knowledge and skill to meet them.

The lack of professional training in modern non-profits is inexcusable, but there may be many reasons for its absence: the ministry might not have sufficient funds for training; managers may think that skills are best passed on through a kind of institutional osmosis; they may believe that time away from day-to-day tasks for training is time wasted; they may simply not want to spend the money. At worst, they may think that equipping people to do superior work is a threat to their own job stability. Whatever the reason, failing to help your co-workers upgrade and improve their professional skills impoverishes them and your organization.

The training mindset is marked by *three sacrifices*: money, time, and accountability. Staff training is usually expensive, and the costs do not always show an immediate return on investment. There are also opportunity costs. It means taking time out of the work week to send your people to training sessions, conferences and seminars. Even when you bring in specialists for in-house training, it means releasing associates from their immediate duties so they can attend the training. Increasing knowledge and skills always costs something.

Training as a specific type of human investment can be much more valuable to an organization than its financial portfolio. Training has very positive medium- and long-term effects on the organization by augmenting skills and capacities that are used for making your mission more effective in the long term.

Then again, sometimes the returns are immediate. The associate who becomes more proficient at using a complex fundraising database today can put his new skills to work on it tomorrow. If that associate stays with the organization for any length of time, he may eventually be able to teach other co-workers the ins and outs of it without having to send them to expensive training sessions off-site.

Accountability is also essential. Leaders and managers must ask questions before they send their associates for training: How will this training benefit the working capacity of So-and-So? What tangible benefit will this training bring to the mission? Is the skill to be acquired part of the associate's job description or within a reasonable range of skills needed for the performance of his job? Above all, *who* will hold So-and-So accountable for results after the training? If supervisors cannot answer these basic questions, they should not make the sacrifices needed for staff training.

Training is only for those who show the promise of increased skill and who have some expectation of longevity with the organization or in the overall movement. Some organizations even have it as their mission to be "training organizations". These groups make it possible, through internships, scholarships, work programs and the like, for their trainees to eventually take on greater roles in the overall movement itself.

The well-named Leadership Institute (LI) in Arlington, Virginia is one such organization. Founded by Morton Blackwell in 1979, the LI very quickly established itself as the preeminent training center for young conservative leaders and flourished during the Reagan years. LI's entire mission is to help young people acquire the principles and skills needed for service in the private or public sectors. I know many dynamic leaders running for- and non-profit companies today who got their start with LI. It remains one of the most effective organizations on the planet with a very strong track record of success to prove its worth.

Train your people. Don't neglect this necessary leadership priority. It will pay you and your mission back in spades.

5. *Flow Chart Discipline*

This catchy term comes from the main tool that businesses use to show how jobs relate to one another in an organization (the flow chart). It also describes the difficulty of keeping all the parts of a mission working together efficiently. That task requires discipline. Consider the following seven elements of flow chart discipline:

Hire For the Job, Not the Person

Non-profit leaders sometimes give in to the temptation of *creating new* positions for individuals just because they have talent or because they are good people in need of a job.

Never do this.

An organization hires people for *its own* distinct *mission needs*, never for any individual's personal needs, as sympathetic as a leader might be to these. Only rarely should you consider a prospective employee's intelligence or talent as primary factors in hiring. They are factors of course, but, as stated in the last chapter, leaders hire for performance, and more specifically, for the unique performance capacities that their organization needs.

Make it a professional courtesy to respond, however perfunctorily, to people who send resumes or inquire about employment, letting them know that your organization hires *only* when there are open positions and hires only those who have the requisite qualifications for the job advertised. That way, inquirers understand that you run a performance organization, not a well-intentioned ministry. Keep hard copy and/or electronic resumes for future review when jobs become available. Someone whose skills are not needed today may be ideal for an open position tomorrow.

No Nebulous Job Descriptions

Every job in the organization should have an updated job description that *fits* the *actual* performance requirements for that position. Everyone in the organization should be able to explain clearly how they personally create value for the mission. Associates have to be crystal clear about what the organization needs and what it expects them to do for the mission.

A highly specific job description is the basis for hiring, but after that, periodically, an associate should work with his supervisor to adapt it for changing circumstances or developing capacities. Together they may emphasize or eliminate certain elements of the job description to increase the strength of the associate's performance as long as the adaptation doesn't change the fundamental job or skew it away from the actual needs of the mission.

In crafting job descriptions, avoid nebulous language and vague descriptions of the job's requirements. These written expectations do not need to be extensive, but they need to be highly specific about responsibilities, both as a guide to focused work and as a tool for yearly evaluations.

Performance Objectives and Evaluations

Along with the job description, each associate should set performance goals and itemized results that he or she can be held accountable for in their jobs. These goals are based on the needs of the mission, *not* on what the employee likes or does not like to do. They should be written down after consultation with supervisors. The leader and the associate should have a common understanding of what excellent performance in that position should look like. Of course, there is always lamentation about the dreaded yearly performance evaluation, but it is not my purpose here to question it. Many others have written extensively about its benefits and deficits. Our point is that some form of goal-setting and regular assessment is needed for every position, including that of the top leader (normally by the board).

No Automatic Raises

Some associates believe that good evaluations should result in automatic raises – no! "Wage inflation" becomes unmanageable for an organization over time if every good worker receives a raise every year for performing his job well. Aren't missionaries *expected* to perform well – always? Top performance is what a performance organization pays people to deliver.

Ask an associate who expects regular salary increases this question: Using the same logic, should we also dock pay for *mediocre* performance? That puts the issue into greater perspective for most people.

Raises and incentives are part of a healthy performance culture, but they should be parceled out according to objective standards, not on a schedule or with feel-good criteria. Most organizations need some sort of Salary Management Program[4] for the purposes of taking the burden off managers who are likely to be subjective in their judgments about these things. A performance culture should *reward* superior performance, but leaders should dampen all expectations of receiving raises after good performance evaluations. It's an unsustainable practice and sends the wrong message.

All Work Must Be Assigned

The leader should make sure that all the work of an organization is assigned *to someone*, whether that work is the standard fare of the mission or some new project the organization is taking on. Drucker again: "No decision has been made until someone is designated to carry it out. Someone has to be accountable – with a work plan, a goal, and a deadline. Decisions don't make themselves effective; people do."[5]

---

[4] Here is a great resource: Jerry Jensen, "Salary Management for Nonprofits: The Fine Art of Distributing Dissatisfaction Equitably," The Grantsmanship Center (www.tgci.com), easily found on the Web.

[5] This was a major concern of Peter Drucker in *Managing the Non-Profit Organization: Principles and Practices* (NY: HarperBusiness, 1992), 128.

A leader must say specifically to an associate, "Jim, this is now your job," or discuss with him how he is going to be able to accomplish a new task in the overall scheme of his workload. Will he need to shift tasks or delegate current responsibilities to someone else to take on the new work? Does the associate need specific types of support or resources to be successful at this new task? A leader should never set his co-workers up for failure.

That is how work gets done in an organization. Vague generalizations and good intentions about doing work are not plans. Every task must have someone's name on it or the organization should not take on a new project. When these assignments are parceled out with specific guidelines or goals, they also signal to associates that they will be held accountable for specific results when it comes time for evaluation.

Effective Use of Contractors

Leaders should hire contractors for short-term work and tasks that need expertise that the organization may not have. It is usually (but not always) more cost-effective to do so. The organization should not hire for regular positions unless there is a *significant amount of work to do* on a regular basis to justify the job. Contractors, however, can do needed tasks when these do not fit anyone else's job description or capabilities, or even when some task would take a competent associate away from something of higher priority he should be doing.

Be extremely careful in hiring contractors, however, because they often promise much and deliver little – and sometimes at great expense. The contracting relationship is an "arms-length" relationship that commits the organization to specific work terms but only for a short period of time. Leaders should place very stringent performance expectations on contractors and dismiss them at the least sign of negligence or poor performance. There are too many skilled freelancers out there willing to work hard and apply their skills to your mission for you to waste time on people who don't deliver.

And never hire *friends* as contractors, particularly if they are long-time friends. (Casual friends or lesser acquaintances, maybe.) Friends usually expect favorable treatment or financial benefits simply because they are friends. If you have to get tough with them for lack of performance you've lost both a job and an ally. If you want to keep a good friend, don't hire him. As with hiring family members, every leader needs a coherent policy on this matter.

No Fat in the Operations

For the non-profit organization, overstaffing is worse than understaffing. All the jobs in the organization should be clearly defined, highly challenging, robust and exciting for everyone from the CEO to the custodial help. If an organization has under-challenged people on staff, the results can be harmful: too much discretionary time for gossip, internal politics, pursuing personal agendas on company time, etc.

Leaders should revise, combine, or simply eliminate jobs that aren't challenging. They are not worthy of the mission. Except for proper times off, associates should be very busy, active and motivated, with little or no time to derail the mission into personal or petty issues. They're hired to work. Drucker says that "the mission has to be clear and simple. It has to be bigger than any one person's capacity. It has to lift up people's vision. It has to be something that makes each person feel that he or she can make a difference – that each one can say, I have not lived in vain."[6]

In short, these seven elements of flow chart discipline help the organization to keep its fitness and readiness for the mission. Hire and train performers, keep them busy, keep them

---

[6] Drucker, *Non-Profit*, 149.

focused, and your mission will reap the benefits of consistently high performance.

6. Failing to Plan is Planning to Fail

This organizational principle may be trite, but it is quite true. Leaders have to spend a good deal of time planning for the future while at the same time staying fully grounded in the present. When an organization lacks good planning, it eventually ignores its own priorities and falls prey to the "one day at a time" ethic, which is a good motto for Alcoholics Anonymous, but not for your *organization!*

In the complex world of modern communications, schedules and networks, planning is necessary to accomplish anything of significance. Good planning doesn't have to be a chore. It's more a matter of having the right mindset and institutional discipline to be forward-looking about the mission. Consider these three standard forms of planning:

Strategic Planning

Strategic planning is the complex, multi-faceted, consultative process that brings all stakeholders of an organization into a structured dialogue about the future of the mission. All associates, from board members to the humblest worker, are invited to take part in the planning, in one form or another. Due to all the facets of organizational life that must be taken into account, it is a process that usually lasts several months, either less or more depending on the complexity of the mission. If it is done well, it results in a document outlining the common aspirations and specific plans for organizational growth projected over a multi-year timeframe.

There are so many resources available on this topic it would be futile to try to explain the ins-and-outs of the complex process here. One critical thing a leader must do, however, is to take the temperature of his organization to assess whether or not his people are ready for such a complex planning process. If not, a modest goal-setting process is better in the short-term. Strategic planning aims to assure the long-term survival and productivity of an organization, whether commercial or charitable. Someone once asked the founder of Panasonic, Konosuke Matsushita, how far into the future his company's strategic plan reached, and he famously answered, "350 years." That's a bit much! Whatever the projected time frame, however, all organizations need exceptional leadership to marshal support within the organization for a strategic planning process—and to have the focus and discipline to see it through to its fruition.

Project Planning

Projects are coordinated actions that put into effect some aspect of the mission in a dynamic way. Organizations and their priorities change, but their overall missions don't (at least not as easily as short-term plans do). Something that works today may not work tomorrow; key project managers may fail or move away; popular trends fade; human needs expand and contract; great performers lose their edge. Even the most successful initiatives of mature organizations do not last forever. These are all realities of living in a complex, changing world.

The criteria for project planning are these: a clear alignment of the proposed project with the core mission; realism about funding for it; reasonable enthusiasm to drive it; and ownership of its outcome (usually by a team, sometimes by an individual). If all these elements do not line up, the leader should exercise his veto or remand the project for further planning. Some projects that are put on hold for lack of any one of the above elements may gel in the future and become a staple of an organization's mission. Others are put in the dustbin of good intentions.

One instance of project ownership stands out in my mind. My international non-profit once took on a support project for a group that was campaigning to stop some terrible legislation in another country. The local grassroots campaign we were supporting had no funding or technical support, so we provided it for them. Our project team met and planned the various elements of our support (website and database creation, press releases, funding from our "campaign" reserve, and so forth.)

Before we launched the campaign's website, however, I made it clear to my tech support person that, due to the bitter controversy surrounding the issue in the other country, the consequences of failure could be catastrophic. Then I told him that web security was not only critical, it was a *top* priority. He of course nodded in agreement, but since he had never been to that country or met our allies there, he didn't quite appreciate the intensity of their battle.

Then I looked directly at him and said more pointedly, "Just to be clear: if either the campaign's website or our own information system gets hacked or compromised in any way, *you* will lose your job." His eyes widened, and he suddenly realized that I was deadly serious. I was the more experienced missionary and understood the potential cost of failure. Once *he* became aware of the high stakes involved (for himself as well), he threw himself into the project and performed marvelously!

Projects are tangible ways to accomplish the short-term objectives of your mission, and you should plan them well. Above all, you should assure that no project ever turns into anyone's pet project or that it is based on promises without the prospect of clear results. Don't hesitate to hold people accountable for a project's success.

Budgeting

The annual budgeting process is perhaps the key area where organizational planning touches the lives of all associates. Budgeting is essential to an organization's operational integrity, and leaders need to take it seriously. It is a form of short-term planning, not just a way to parcel out money for programs. As noted earlier (Chapter 1, Point 4), there is a symbiosis between money and mission, and nowhere is that more evident than in budgeting.

The budget preparation process should not be a routine adjustment of categories that remain the same from year to year but, rather, a hands-on process where leaders sit down with workers to evaluate whether or not the activities and expenses of their work match mission priorities. All budget discussions should take into account several critical elements: the associate's experience of the mission; the organization's need to respond to external factors; a realistic assessment of administrative costs; new initiatives and projects that will be relevant in the coming year, etc. These are the nuts and bolts of the mission and find a sort of quantitative expression in budgets.

7. Hire for Work Ethic and Productivity

We touched on these items in the last chapter when we discussed building a performance culture (particularly in Point 5, "Hire and Keep Actual Performers"). The question of work ethic is both personal and institutional. Performers are workers. They might not be worker bee types who arrive and leave at exactly the same time every day and carry out their tasks with mechanical precision, but all real performers have a strong worth ethic and are known by their results. You only want productive workers on your team. Here are a few items to look for in your task of creating a diligent, productive workforce:

Zero Tolerance for Laziness and Nonsense

When a person is hired for the mission, the boss expresses directly to the new hire the reasonable expectation that the associate will "go the extra mile" for the mission when needed. Apostolates do not expect people to be slaves to a job – no mission is an end in itself – but sometimes people have to do things they'd prefer not to do or be inconvenienced in ways they did not expect. They must do them for the sake of the mission, as long as no other vital personal interests are sacrificed. It's their job to do them.

Whiners, complainers, gossipers, narcissists, drama queens (and kings), back stabbers, slackers, dysfunctional and disruptive types, people who refuse to make sacrifices for the overall good when *reasonable* demands of the mission call for them are unsuited for work in a faith-based mission. Get rid of them as soon as you possibly can. They are not missionaries. They are functionaries. Keep only those who have zeal for the work and who are willing to go the extra mile.

Paid to Work

Each salaried associate is paid for a full day's work, defined in American work culture as an eight-hour work day or forty-hour work week. The quantity of hours worked may be more, but it should never be less, excluding authentic health needs or crises. It is a privilege to work for a non-profit mission, and getting paid to do so is an even greater blessing. We are not talking about disrupting normal family life by excessive work demands, of course. We are just establishing an expectation of justice in the workplace.

It is a matter of simple justice to do a day's work for a day's pay. Basic honesty demands that everyone fulfill this moral obligation to the mission. This is more a matter of personal standards than of policies or monitoring. It is a matter of each one's stewardship of the "widow's mite." Laziness, failure to work proper hours, spending time on low-impact matters, giving less than one's best efforts, skimping on time cards, etc. are wastes of donor funds and issues for evaluation. Everyone is paid to work.

Identify Productive Creativity

Many leaders feel threatened by creative people, but human ingenuity is a *vital* force for a vital mission. Despite its sometimes unusual packaging, creativity is always an asset, and a leader seeks it out or at least recognizes it when it shows up.

A vital distinction has to be made here. There are creative types who are talented but narcissistic. These types are generally not worth the effort to manage and should be quickly let go when their high maintenance personalities contribute more complications than value to the organization.

I once inherited two creative types in the communications department of an organization. They were both enormously talented, but the more dysfunctional of the two, who regularly missed deadlines and forgot things, was a real worker and actually produced much greater quality output than the other prima donna who always showed up on time but caused his manager enormous headaches. Guess which of the two creative types kept his job.

Creativity doesn't always come in the stereotype of the artistic persona, and a good leader learns to distinguish between self-promoting narcissists and truly productive creators of any stripe. Leaders hire *creative performers* who are bold in imagining what can be done and who also have a track record of creative success in their respective fields. Just because a person is glib or brimming with ideas or flamboyant does not mean he's a performer. True creative performers produce results, which is the only way to measure creativity. Then, reward them for their creative successes so that they continue to offer their talents and ingenuity to your mission.

Beware of Empty Activity

A strong work ethic is important, but never confuse mere activity with productive work. Simply being busy does not mean your work is effective. The key to productivity is doing "first things first" (Point 2 above) and keeping priorities in place so that empty, busy work will not consume vital energies that are needed for the important work of the mission.

In sum, hiring and personnel decisions are inevitably complex with many hits and misses along the way. Yet, this is an area where the leader must establish his own positive track record. He must learn the crucial skills needed for making good hiring decisions, and he must get perceptibly better at hiring only productive workers. A vital mission is always vitalized by that essential leadership skill.

8. *Manage Your Board*

The final organizational principle has to do with the leader's relationship with his board of directors. A friend of mine once advised me to "manage [my] board" – of which he was a member. That was his way of saying that he wanted a strong leader to be the coordinator of other strong leaders for the good of the organization and mission. For our purposes, my primary reference point will be the relationship between a CEO (or an equivalent position of authority with a different title: President, Executive Director, General Manager, etc.) and his board, but these points may apply analogously to any leader whose position is accountable to someone else's oversight.

Non-profit boards of directors, according to US tax law, are supervisory in nature, not managerial, which is an important difference in function. It means that the responsibilities of the board and the CEO are distinct but interlocking. Ideally, they have a working *partnership in the mission* rather than a power-sharing arrangement, and hopefully never an adversarial relationship.

Roughly speaking, the board exercises supervisory authority over all matters related to the institution and, like the US Senate, holds a type of "advice and consent" function in relation to the chief executive. They are ultimately responsible for overall solidity and security of the organization, but they do not, and should not, inject themselves into the day-to-day operations of the organization.

The CEO is entrusted with the regular functioning of the institution and with executing all administrative decisions that affect its ongoing mission. He is responsible for all immediate financial, fundraising, communications, and missionary decisions even though he doesn't perform all these functions himself. He is the public face of the organization and the prime spokesperson in all matters relating to the mission.

The CEO's relationship with the board, therefore, is one of informing, advising, and even lobbying for particular mission interests. His *modus operandi* should be scrupulous honesty, full disclosure about all issues of importance, good communication, and strict accountability. He does not need to run every administrative decision by them or seek their advice on routine matters, however. The quarterly board meeting is the forum where the legal stewards of the institution make decisions for the good of the mission, but to do so, they need to be informed by the CEO of every critical element of the organization's life.

On matters that have to do with legal compliance, corporate policy, large financial concerns, or crisis management, the CEO must always consult the board. Whether to hire or fire a staff member, for example, is his decision, but whether to hire or fire corporate legal counsel or make a huge financial outlay is a matter to run by the board of directors. Both CEO and board may need time to understand the limits of their distinct areas of responsibility – it is a human relationship, after all – but all should strive to avoid some of the following common pitfalls that affect the CEO/board relationship:

Politics

The CEO should try to create trust and keep internal politics to a minimum by good communications with the board as a whole and also with key individual members. Everyone likes to be kept informed. On any critical issues or crises, the board should hear things directly from the CEO, immediately, before they hear anything through the grapevine. His diligence about board communication keeps them abreast of happenings and prevents politics, rumors and innuendo from negatively affecting their working relationship.

Over-Involvement with Staff

Disgruntled associates may seek sympathy by appealing directly to individual board members. Staff-to-board communication is a *very bad idea* except in specifically delegated matters. Even then, it should normally be the responsibility of one point person in the organization who the CEO tasks to handle those matters. The leader should instruct associates how to follow the chain of command in addressing problems and of course policy manuals should lay out proper procedures for this.

Board-to-staff contact should likewise be kept to a minimum. The CEO should inform board members that, except for legitimate whistle-blowing concerns as laid out in corporate policy, the board should not pay attention to or involve themselves in the work-related affairs of associates, nor return any communications without the CEO's knowledge.

The same holds true if the organization has retained legal counsel for any reason. During one difficult period at a non-profit, I had disgruntled associates calling our lawyer to complain about this and that, and the lawyer was happy to keep the clock running while he racked up billable hours for that month. I put a swift end to that practice when I informed the lawyer that I intended to *bill him* for any future contact he had with members of our regular staff.

These policies are not power plays on the part of the CEO. They are healthy boundaries he puts in place to manage important relationships up and down the chain.

Micromanagement and Neglect

The CEO's sphere of authority lies in running the regular affairs of the organization, and the board should generally allow him to do things his way without too much interference or questioning of his judgment. If the board consistently loses confidence in his way of handling the business of the organization, they are entirely within their rights to dismiss him and hire another who will do it more to their liking.

On the other hand, the CEO has a sacred duty to consult board members on matters that affect the well-being of the institution or mission. The board is usually a reservoir of life experience, business acumen, and practical, human wisdom that can be the CEO's greatest asset. He should not neglect their wisdom and not pretend he has all the answers all the time.

Fundraising Function

The CEO has the major burden of fundraising, but he must also hold the board accountable for helping to increase the financial strength of the institution. This is true for *all* board members. They are the primary custodians of its wellbeing. The wealthier board members should be big donors to the mission; others of lesser means should use their networks and influence to bring in new donors; some may even give in-kind gifts through their valuable professional services and advice.

Case in point: a board member of mine was a lawyer by profession and may have made the single greatest contribution to our organization by his years of pro-bono legal counsel. His trenchant legal advice kept our organization compliant with changing laws and regulations and, perhaps more importantly, kept us out of legal quandaries for more than a decade. Whatever their way of contributing, all board members should help shoulder the difficult task of financially sustaining the mission.

Choosing Board Members

This final board management item is perhaps the most important. The CEO is the person who normally selects and presents potential board members for a vote. Board members may also present worthy candidates for consideration. The criteria for board membership are several: the candidate should have a heart for the mission and show an existing commitment to the cause; the candidate should be a person of means and influence, or one who can strengthen the financial position of the organization in some way; and the candidate should share the core values of the mission. It also helps if the candidate shares the vision of the CEO, but that is not a primary concern. The CEO needs dissenting voices on his board as well.

Board management is a delicate balancing act, but leaders who effectively manage board members for the tremendous human assets they are, will run the most effective organizations. Dynamic missions *inevitably* flourish from a healthy relationship between both partners.

Conclusion

Non-profit organizations exist to organize human efforts and resources into a dynamic force for change. This change always seeks the betterment of people and their conditions, but non-profit leaders can undermine their own cause if they ignore certain fundamental principles of organization. Strong leaders get good institutional organization skills down early and implement them so they waste as little as possible of their donors' funds, staff time, and resources on a drawn-out learning curve.

Each of the principles discussed in this chapter has to do with people and disciplined habits, but none of them have to do with any personal benefit to the leader, except in the eyes of the Lord we serve. Blessed are the leaders and the missions that can put these principles into effect!

Chapter 5

Core Performance Principles

1. "It Never Gets Easier—Ever"

2. Good Intentions Don't Pay the Bills

3. Networking and Phone Time

4. Build a Cathedral

5. Always Remember the "Core Unit"

6. Two Essential Performance Disciplines

7. Hone Your Skills

8. Balance and Time Out

*Life is a game of cards. The hand that is dealt you
represents determinism; the way you play it is free will.*

~*Jawaharlal Nehru*

1. *"It Never Gets Easier—Ever"*

The reason I've put this principle in quotation marks is
because it's a direct quote from a board member who took me
aside after my first board meeting at a new job and told me that
I should never expect leading such a large organization to be
easy. He said the responsibilities will always have a claim on me,
and they will never let up for the entire time I hold that office.

The board member was not known for his subtlety! But he
was wise. Very wise. He was a former insurance company CEO
who knew what it meant to have the weight of responsibility
on his shoulders for years, and his advice remains durable
across all types of organizations. There are "hard" and "soft"
responsibilities for everyone in authority, and a leader has to
learn to live with both.

The hard ones start the day you get hired.

The first hard pressure for a leader is the legal responsibility
he takes on when elected. The board is the legal owner of the
non-profit and has ultimate legal accountability for it. The CEO,
however, has *immediate* accountability for all the goings-on of
his team and institution. In civil law it's called *liability,* and the
CEO wears it as a heavy yoke around his neck at all times.

If the organization is sued for anything, legitimate or not,
the person in charge is the one who has to go to court. If the
organization has to answer inquiries and audits, summonses
and petitions, the buck stops on his desk. If someone in the
administration misses a filing deadline or a compliance
requirement, the leader pays the price. Sometimes opportunists
and enemies try to exploit the organization's weaknesses or set

it up for a lawsuit, and the leader is the fall guy. No, it never gets easier.

The second hard responsibility is *fundraising*. If the fundraising team doesn't bring in enough money to pay the bills, who gets blamed? The top guy. Whether fairly or not, employees, project managers and affiliates look to him as the one to provide financial security for them at all times, especially during economic downturns. His name is on their paychecks. Sometimes they expect him to produce money out of thin air.

A leader will often have to be the bad guy who injects a sense of fiscal realism into the organization's operations. He generally does the financial belt-tightening and is the one who gets suspicious looks when he spends money that others might think would be better spent elsewhere (on *their* projects, of course). It's a hard job, but someone has to do it. That someone is you.

A third hard responsibility is the constant work of *PR and public speaking*. The person in charge is always giving talks to some audience, large or small. There is no let-up in pressure to perform well, whether it is in front of a stadium full of activists, a TV audience, his own team members, or people who pigeonhole him in Dunkin Donuts. From the time he leaves home in the morning until the moment he crashes into bed at night, he is in the public eye, he is Johnny-on-the-spot, solving every problem, providing every answer, in touch with every trend, prepared for all contingencies, expected to answer every communication and attend every event, vanquishing every enemy, able to leap tall buildings in a single bound, etc. The hard pressures of the job don't have strict upper limits; and they never get easier.

"Soft" responsibilities are only easier in that they have less immediacy or stress attached to them, but they are no less persistent. Among these: his ongoing need to cultivate personal virtue and see to his own professional development as well as that of his own team. He must network with other leaders in the movement; maintain a presence at key social events; balance his spiritual, family, and work responsibilities; produce quality output for the mission and execute flawless follow-up on all projects, great or small. He's expected to remain up-to-date on macro issues and trends that affect his field, to stay in touch with local issues and concerns, to be aware of all issues concerning his associates as well as his own friends and extended family, etc. These are just for starters.

Sure, "it never gets easier", but leadership is an incredibly rewarding life. No one in his right mind would trade the pressures for anything else.

2. *Good Intentions Don't Pay the Bills*

For every individual who pays attention to budgets, cash flow, financial audits and spreadsheets, there are five more who have good intentions about money but don't understand how it works in a non-profit. (Truth be told, many people don't have a clue about how *their personal* finances work either.) If they think about anything other than their own paycheck, they generally presume that the ministry has more money than it actually does. They don't have the fiscal realism of the people in charge of paying the bills. This is even truer for affiliates in foreign countries who only see pots of money at the end of a rainbow wherever Americans are concerned.

The leader has to teach his associates fiscal realism. He must show them what it means to live within their organizational means, which of course are larger than personal or family finances, but still limited. The best way to develop fiscal realism is to ask coworkers to calculate ahead of time the *total cost* for a desired purchase or project of theirs before it goes beyond the idea stage. This activity involves time and research, but is one of the best tools a leader has in his fiscal realism toolbox.

This exercise shows people how much the proverbial devil gets into the details of any plan. When associates begin to itemize all aspects of a given project – material costs, travel expenses, production and people costs, including the labor costs of salaried staff – it always comes as a shock to them that *labor* is not actually *free*. Contracts, wages, and prorated costs of salaried members on a project basis must all be factored into the bottom line. The itemization exercises force them to consider these stark realities that leaders deal with daily.

They must also learn to identify *hidden* costs, and that means leaving nothing out of the final tally: taxes and surcharges, mysterious supplemental fees, hidden penalties, transfer fees, the "assessments" that get tacked onto products and services, government regulatory costs, etc. Regarding the latter, I vividly recall an officious little man arriving from the county government on a certain day every year, spending a total of maybe forty-five seconds "inspecting" our elevator and walking out the door with $150 of our hard-earned money. The organization had no choice but to pay the government extortion. Associates should also meet government inspectors from time to time.

Most people don't think about these things because their personal finances don't include special institutional costs. When *they* have to do the rigorous analysis, however, associates begin to "see" the economic dimension of a project with much clearer eyes than in the abstractions of their earth-shattering new ideas and all the fuzzy feelings and good intentions that go with the latest world-transforming venture.

The exercise isn't over. Once the detailed fiscal calculation is done, the "value" discussion takes over with some of the value questions we detailed in the last chapter: "Is this project on-mission?" "Can we do it less expensively and achieve the same result?" "Does God want us to do this?" and so forth.

The act of quantifying the actual cost of their dreams forces associates to acknowledge the intimate connection between money and mission. They begin to see that the most critical discussions are not really about how much something costs but about the *purpose* of the project related to mission (the money/mission symbiosis again). That, in turn, helps them remember the sacrifices that others have made to afford them the opportunity to spend that money on realistic mission priorities.

I noted earlier that there can sometimes be a subtle sense of entitlement among altruistic people who see the value of their own mission and wonder why other people don't see it too and just pony up. They have to learn that good intentions don't pay the bills.

Fundraising and promotions only happen when someone does them. As a rule, they are sheer hard work. The leader with initiative, the one who is willing to beg and present his message to others, is the one who reaps the harvest. We rely on faith in fundraising too, of course, but it's always best not to rely on *miracles* as a fundraising plan. God can, and sometimes does, miraculously fill your coffers – I once received a $100,000 no-strings-attached donation out of the blue – but God doesn't normally suspend the laws of economics to save us from our lack of diligence in this area.

Sometimes begging means getting criticized for being overly-focused on money. So be it. I once met the man who invented direct mail fundraising, Richard Viguerie, who told me that he regularly received a stack of complaint letters from people griping about him sending out too many begging letters. All came from Christians worried about poor stewardship and wasteful use of funds, etc. Viguerie then showed me that stack of complaints sitting next to the stack of envelopes with *checks* that came from the same mailing, and the income stack was at least three times higher!

There is a basic law of economics we all must respect: you have to spend money to make money. And that is not bad stewardship.

Here is another harsh fundraising truism: cash doesn't grow on trees. It has to be generated. Good intentions will never make dollars flutter down like stardust from heaven. So, first get on your knees and then get up and get to work!

3. *Networking and Phone Time*

No one can be an effective leader unless he spends a great deal of time talking to people, making contacts and attending meetings. In the modern age, this means spending a massive amount of time on the phone doing all the boring or routine networking tasks that bring people together. A leader knows that the people on the other end of the phone are his allies in the mission, but sometimes the burden of phone time is a great cross for a leader to carry, especially if he is an introvert.

Building and maintaining a network of allies is hard work: building databases of names and addresses; keeping those lists updated; following up on requests and favors; calling people to renew contacts; setting up meetings and meals; seeking counsel, etc. These are the substance of good networking and they pay large dividends in fortifying our mission.

There are two downsides to networking, though. The first is that when you ask people for favors, they often ask for something in return, and sometimes they ask for more than you can give. We all depend on the assistance of others for our projects, but that means we have to give back – and I've never known anyone to call in a favor at a convenient time. As I noted previously, we hardly have time for our own projects let alone the good projects of others. We need prudence and great skill to help others achieve their goals without losing focus on our own.

The second problem is that, despite the number of times you do favors for others, when *you* need something, the same people often fail you. Networking involves risk-taking that sometimes leaves you holding the bag.

Nonetheless, strong networks are a sort of gold standard for all effective leaders. When I assumed the leadership of a large non-profit a few years ago, I found in a drawer a multi-page printout entitled "Contacts", which turned out to be a copy of the networking database of the organization's retired founder. It didn't take long to realize what an immensely influential man he had been through his contacts. He clearly worked his list because we knew that most of the leaders on that list regularly showed up at his events! I have seen well-connected leaders who can call a number of key allies in their database on a moment's notice to get help with anything they need. Strive for that kind of networking strength.

4. *Build a Cathedral*

Mark Twain thought that compound interest was the most powerful force in the world. He didn't mean that in just a financial sense, although money investments certainly have that power. He was referring to the power of building something greater than the sum of its parts, of building something of great value that can only be constructed patiently one block, one element at a time and according to a larger plan. Persevering effort of this type unleashes a powerful force on the world for good.

Twain would contrast his assertion with the lifeless power of cyclical effort, i.e., repeating the same task over and over again without a vision for something greater. Everyone can appreciate the difference between a man who has thirty years of experience in a job and a man who has one year of experience – thirty times.

That image captures, in missionary terms, why building a cathedral is a vastly greater achievement than building endless lines of cheap row houses all with the same floor plan. A leader wants to build a one-of-a-kind cathedral of his mission, but that takes time, effort and much cumulative brickwork.

Much has been made of the now-famous 1993 study by Swedish psychologist, K. Anders Ericsson, which suggested that a person who wants to achieve mastery in any field must spend at least 10,000 hours of his life just *practicing* and honing a talent.[1] Our non-profit missionary purposes may be less ambitious, but most leaders and great entrepreneurs also achieve great successes by spending thousands of hours along the way focusing on one thing of great value, their own Pearl of Great Price (Matthew 13:45-46).

Mission work is about building something of value in the world that was not there before, something durable in the human community that creates the kind of change for good that the mission promises. We are not talking here about building physical structures (although these may sometimes be elements of a leader's vision) but rather of building human and social structures in a metaphorical sense. Networks and ministries are built. Communities and educational institutions are built. Careers, programs, movements and organizations are all built by someone with a vision.

Their builders create each of these structures with great diligence and according to a plan, even if that plan isn't fully formed at its inception or develops organically over time. Even Ed Catmull, co-founder of the amazing Pixar Digital Animation Studios, had this to say about creative "vision" which is not always in high-definition when creators begin their work:

> I've known many people I consider to be creative geniuses, and not just at Pixar and Disney, yet I can't remember a single one who could articulate exactly what this vision

---

[1] Cited by Keller, *The ONE Thing*, 177; the study was published in the journal *Psychological Review* (1993) and is entitled, "The Role of Deliberate Practice in the Acquisition of Expert Performance." This study was also featured in other books on expertise, including Malcolm Gladwell's, *The Tipping Point*; Geoff Colvin's, *Talent is Overrated*; Angela Duckworth's, *Grit*, among others.

was that they were striving for when they started. In my experience, creative people discover and realize their visions over time and through dedicated, protracted struggle. In that way, creativity is more like a marathon than a sprint. You have to pace yourself.[2]

There is also the example of the Mayo Clinic, which started as a response to a natural disaster. Famed motivational speaker Zig Ziglar told the story of the humble origins of the now-mighty institution:

> Mother Alfred Moes, the founder of the Sisters of St. Francis, brought her untrained nuns to assist in nursing those who had been injured in the tornado. While there, she convinced the leading town doctor to head an unbuilt hospital she would raise the funds to construct. That physician and surgeon's name was William Worral May and the hospital, St. Mary's, was the forerunner to and still affiliated with the world-famous Mayo Clinic[3].

The rest is history, as they say.

Some plans for world-changing projects burst wholly-formed into the mind of visionary leaders. These are rare though. Others come from strategic planning processes. Most people, however, start with a passionate personal interest, a talent or gift in their hearts that has an orientation toward service. Then they build it up, incrementally, into a change movement, an institution, a transformative ministry, a beautiful work. Above all, the building process is slow, immensely challenging, and easily derailed. Its builder/creator needs perseverance, focus,

---

[2]   Ed Catmull, *Creativity, Inc.: Overcoming the Unseen Forces That Stand in the Way of True Inspiration* (NY: Random House, 2014), 222.

[3]   Zig Ziglar, *Something to Smile About* (Thomas Nelson: Nashville, 1997), 63; citing a 1996 article in *Investors Daily*.

ingenuity, and dogged determination over a long period of time to see it to completion.

Building projects of any type are that way. They usually start with a grand ideal, a concept, a passionate desire to produce something of value, and they go through stages of growth and expansion before they reach maturity. What is undeniably true about any creative process, however, is that it is incremental. The cathedral image is apt. It's always a long, long process. Cologne Cathedral in Germany took *six hundred years* to complete!

An *ineffective* leader goes about routine things without ever seeing the inherent connectedness of all those actions in a larger plan. He does the same things over and over again and often just rearranges the deck chairs on the *Titanic*, to reprise the opening image of this book. The effective leader, on the other hand, holds his creative vision in his mind each day and adds one element, one brick at a time to his creation, as a way of compounding interest in his project over time.

The danger is that you will let your vision be *dissipated or your passion derailed* by trivial requests, interruptions, low-priority tasks, and disorganization. The scatter-shot approach only works in skeet shooting. A leader must concentrate his creative vision like a magnifying glass that gathers and focuses the rays of the sun to burn a hole in a piece of paper. And do that for many years.

To build a cathedral, you must be intensely focused on your creative priorities but also keep them to a minimum. Peter Drucker had a famous saying that the person who gets things done is like "a monomaniac with a mission." You have to be that kind of monomaniac if you want to leave a significant gift of grace to the world. Through the cumulative power of time and deliberate effort, and with the help of many allies over the years, you will eventually build a glorious cathedral.

5. *Always Remember the "Core Unit"*

Every organization needs vast amounts of resources (read: money) to stay alive, and resources are always limited. In Chapter 3 we said that we do not advocate the unnecessary duplication of services or unhealthy competition between non-profit organizations. Here we are talking less about what other people do and more about the need to be highly proactive about acquiring needed resources to run *your* mission. Your greatest competition for resources is really your own lack of diligence in pursuing them.

Leaders never lose sight of their basic "core unit" of economic survival, which drives an organization's mission in good times and keeps it going in hard times. In the non-profit world, the core unit is the individual donor.

Every field of human endeavor has a core unit that is the essential bedrock of their financial and public support. The categories are fairly simple to discern. In business, the core unit is the customer; in government, it is the taxpayer; in the Church, it is the parishioner; in sports, it is the fan; in entertainment, it is the audience; and in the non-profit world, again, I emphasize, it is the donor.

Every organization pays attention to, invests in, and strengthens its outreach to its own core unit, or it withers. Without them it can't even operate, let alone thrive in rough economic environments. Let's examine a few ways the faith-based leader manages and builds up his organization's support base. The following are a few simple donor relations techniques:

Constant Gratitude

Individual donors come in all shapes and sizes; every non-profit will also have groups, foundations, businesses, and other organizations that contribute to the cause. They are essential to the wellbeing of the mission, and you cannot thank them enough for their contributions, large or small. Personal phone calls, postcards when travelling, handwritten notes, public recognition (with the donor's permission), and constant gratitude whenever you meet them lets them know that their sacrifices are appreciated. Everyone feels in their hearts the extent of their own sacrifice for your cause, and they need to hear – regularly, and from the top – that it is appreciated.

A Numbers Game

A faith-based mission is all about values and quality, but donor relations is strictly a numbers game. To be somewhat crass about it, *more donors translates into more funding*, and that cannot be denied. (Recall the two stacks of envelopes in Point 2 above.) However, the real financial prospects of an organization lie in the long-term work of *donor retention* – encouraging donors to stay with the mission in good times and bad, to give proportionally more each year, and to become their own network of influence by passing on news, literature and enthusiasm about your mission to others. There is undeniable strength in numbers.

Donor Attrition

Every organization has to face the hard reality of donor attrition. Donors fall away for a variety of reasons: they may be mad at you; they may have lost their job or their shirt in the stock market; they may have kids in college and rising family costs; other organizations may have stolen them; or they may simply have lost interest in the mission. Whatever the reasons, recognize that the donor database is as subject to the law of inertia as any element of the natural world. It does not grow on its own. In fact, it usually shrinks on its own unless you fight the downward slide of donor attrition by list-building and good donor relations – it's a lot of hard work for the person in charge.

Constantly Build Lists

Fundraising and networking is a matter of lists: contact lists, mailing lists, email lists, top donor lists, prospecting lists, events lists, foundation lists, etc. Prospecting for new donors and list-building is often expensive, but it can't be neglected. That is true for each and every one of the lists. If they're not being worked and augmented, they'll decompose and become obsolete and will eventually be useless for the mission. Set benchmarks for your promotional and fundraising associates, work the lists, strive to increase the numbers every year. One of the most popular email services today is called *Constant Contact* – it is well-named. Keeping in constant contact with donors and supporters is an essential leadership quality.

Personal Approach to the Top Percentage

One leader cannot possibly manage hundreds or thousands of active donors, so the Pareto Principle (aka, the 80/20 Principle) applies here. If 80% of the organization's funds come from the top 20% of donors, spend your time on the top one-fifth of your donor list without "losing the common touch."[4] It's as simple as that. A good leader pays attention to his top donors, calls them, visits them, and goes out of his way to help them as much as he is able. Fundraising is personal; people give to people, not to faceless organizations. A leader gives personal attention, within reason, to that portion of his supporters who can write big checks. Certainly, every donor is important to the mission, but as your list grows, personal contact with everyone is impossible. Lean on your supportive associates who can take good care of the other 80%.

---

[4]   From Rudyard Kipling's famous poem, "If".

But...Don't Sacrifice the Mission For a Donor

There inevitably comes a time when an individual donor wants the organization to take on his pet project in exchange for a large donation. All such requests should be prudently considered in light of the mission priorities of the organization, but you should never try to shoehorn someone else's off-mission project into your essential mission just to score a large donation. Deal with every such request respectfully and discern the terms of it carefully. If you and your advisors judge that the request doesn't fit the mission, the answer should be a respectful but definitive "No thank you". Sometimes you can convince the donor to re-align his donation to be more in line with your mission's priorities, but never sacrifice the purity of the mission just to get a big check.

Build Long-Term Support

The ultimate goal of all donor relations is the development of lifetime donors, even *donor families,* who stay with the organization as it matures over the years. Discussions about the "lifetime value" of donors and their families are very helpful for strategic planning purposes. Donors who stay with an organization for a long time are also more likely to leave legacy gifts (wills and bequests) which help build the institutional strength and longevity of an organization.

In sum, the mandate of this performance principle is simple: be diligent about your "core unit" of support. Your donors make it possible for you and your people to do the mission. Pray for them constantly and always thank God that He provides for your mission's needs through such generous souls.

6. *Two Essential Performance Disciplines*

We've already spoken of many types of discipline that you need in order to be an effective leader. This section focuses on the two performance disciplines necessary to become a *tested* leader: reliability and predictability. These disciplines are two sides of the same coin of leadership integrity.

Reliability

Reliability describes the leader who shows up on time, keeps his word, makes proper responses to crises, never fails to meet his responsibilities, and always exceeds demands. It is the leader's awareness that other people depend upon him for many intangible things, not just a paycheck. It is the understanding of who he *is* for other people; that he is a real, living, responsible *presence* in their lives; that his *being there* strengthens them for the hard work of the mission.

Reliability requires a leader to fully embrace his public and vocational duties without complaint, without seeking credit or appreciation. Nothing is ever about you as a leader. It's always about them, those you are called to serve. You are committed to being there for them to the very end of your tenure, giving of your abilities without compromise, even if it means having to make supreme sacrifices to fulfill your duty. Others should describe your reliability in terms like these: he is adamant, persevering, unflagging, careful, discerning, faithful, consistent and reliable as the dawn.

If reliability were an object, it would be a rock. People set the foundations of buildings on rock; they stand tall on a rock to look out at the horizon; and they can even lay out a picnic basket and have a meal on a large, smooth rock. The rock won't be very comfortable or exciting, but it will always be there, immovable and solid when all the world around it seems to be shifting.

I once knew a highly successful seminary rector who wanted to go back to parish work. After he decided to step down, the seminary asked him to stay on as the *temporary spiritual director.* Lesser men would have taken this as an insult and a demotion, but this man agreed to do it as a service to the young men he had supported for many years in his more grandiose capacity. The new rector then kept him on one year longer than planned, and he remained there without the slightest interference with the new rector's policies or decisions.

Finally his superiors gave him a church, but since the seminary was in the middle of its academic year, he did not take up his new assignment right away. He wanted to assure his colleagues and young directees that there would be no lapse in his mission to them, emphasizing that he would remain at the seminary fulfilling his duties "to the very end" (quoting Jesus's words in John 13:1). Until the last seminarian left for summer break, he remained faithful to his commission. *That* is reliability.

Predictability

Good leadership also requires reliability's twin brother, *predictability.* We live in a culture of constant change. Insecurity needs stability. Imbalance needs equilibrium. Uncertainty needs predictability. A leader's predictability provides refuge for the anxieties and indecision of people caught up in a perpetual motion culture.

Predictability doesn't mean a leader must have the answer to every problem or the perfect response to every crisis. It means he is grounded in principles of right action and solid habits that people can anticipate and rely on when needed.

Most people think spontaneity and free-wheeling independence are the greatest expressions of freedom. A leader doesn't. He doesn't mind being a boring non-celebrity figure. He wants to be predictable so that the people who depend on him will have a compass to steer a course through the chaos that all the spontaneous people in society create. To have a predictable leader is a rare gift for any organization, business, family, or community.

When the famed pundit Pat Buchanan wrote his autobiography, *Right From the Beginning*, prior to his presidential run in 1988, he said that one of his greatest achievements was to be able to look back over a thirty-year career as a public figure, and see virtually no change in any conservative position he had held since the 1950s. It's not that he couldn't change his mind – he's one of the most intelligent and perceptive public figures alive – but that his fundamental convictions were extremely realistic and had endured the test of time. Whatever a person may think of Buchanan, it's clear that he had not built his house on shifting sands.

Predictability is, as we've said, a rather unexciting virtue. It doesn't win popularity contests. If reliability is a rock, predictability is a public *monument* whose messages and values are chiseled on its face for all to see. Anyone can walk up to it and read the message that will not change because it is written in stone. A monument is a witness to something that transcends time. It is a fixed marker standing tall in the public square commemorating meaningful events or personages that have had an effect on a community. It becomes part of the landscape, so it's easy to miss, but it remains a point of reference for that community. It is a landmark that orients and directs people to their destinations.

Reliability and predictability are essential leadership virtues, but like any habit, they are acquired only at the cost of time and persistent application. Taken together, they make a leader *trustworthy*. Trust is not given, it is won. It can only be built over time and through consistent habits of honesty and integrity. If you establish your leadership on these twin rocks, people will follow you to the ends of the earth.

7. *Hone Your Skills*

In Stephen Covey's motivational book, *The Seven Habits of Highly Successful People,* he calls this principle "Sharpening the Saw" and describes it as "the principle of continuous improvement."[5] It is the belief that any skill set or human capacity must be reinforced and strengthened, or it atrophies. The Gospel says the same thing: "To him who has, more will be given; from him who has not, what little he has will be taken away from him" (Matthew 13:10-12).

Everyone brings skills to a leadership role. We each have raw talents as well as some refined ones. It is imperative for the leader to know what his own personal gifts are and to continuously develop them in order to perform with ever greater levels of excellence in his mission. The board of directors doesn't choose a leader without deficits – such leaders don't exist. They hire a leader *despite* his deficits and for what he can do for the organization and mission.

On the other hand, a leader should also be humble enough to identify any personal deficits that may reduce or threaten his job performance. He should take steps to fill in his own personal and professional gaps. When he identifies any clear deficit in knowledge or skill related to his direct responsibilities, he sharpens his saw, hones his skills, takes the necessary steps to acquire the needed capacity. The responsibility for building competence is his.

Skill development happens only when you *receive regular and objective feedback* from those who have expertise in the particular area in which you want to grow. Professional training, feedback and coaching are time-consuming and costly, but there is no other way to assure that you're reaching for a higher standard. You may get a lot of quick pats on the

---

5   Stephen R. Covey, *Principle-Centered Leadership* (New York: Free Press, 1991), 275-276.

back from friends and allies who hear you speak in public, but very few of those will give you *honest* feedback about your performance. Trainers generally don't have that limitation.

Hire people from outside the organization to help you because subordinates and co-workers aren't free to engage in that level of honesty with their boss or co-workers. Periodically you have individuals in your organization who by temperament will let you have it with both barrels (usually the ones with the greatest job security.) They are precious resources, but rare! The main point is that we need another pair of eyes, someone who knows what he is talking about, to help us improve at anything. Among all the skills needed to be a good leader, consider the following three types of leadership skill that always need continuous improvement:

Media Savvy

If you have a public profile, you're likely to interact with print and broadcast media to get your message out. Media skills are not innate to most people. In fact, most people abhor the very thought of going in front of a camera. But your position may not leave you a choice in dealing with the media, in some capacity, for the good of your mission. To develop media skills, you need training. Thankfully, there are many techniques for correctly handling both favorable and hostile interviewers, and you don't have to reinvent the wheel. Just learn the techniques bought at the price of much trial and error by other leaders, and don't hesitate to ask for ongoing help to refine your skills.

Writing

You should be constantly writing something. Get your opinions and your organization's positions out in front of people regularly. It is good to have at least one person who functions as an editor for your writing, someone who makes himself available to you when needed and who will review your work before it goes out. Two fresh sets of eyes are even better, but be careful not to ask for *too much* feedback, otherwise you may lose your unique perspective and voice in writing. Master the various written genres that are appropriate to your position: articles, press releases, professional reports, even books, if necessary. By means of writing, you also build your knowledge base, and in so doing, you set down for posterity clear documentation of your leadership expertise.

Management Skill

As noted at the beginning of this book, your job is leadership, but the best leaders have strong managerial skills too. Certain temperaments are more suited to the science of management, but even so, a leader must read and become conversant with the thinking of good managers. Read all of the best management materials available (Peter Drucker!) and subscribe to some of the incredible publications coming out of the management and self-help industry today. Strive to become more objective in your style of management; that is, try to adopt the "best practices" of the industry and adapt these practices to your particular circumstances and mission.

When Stephen Covey pointed out that you need to sharpen the saw, he was saying that you need well-maintained tools to stay up-to-date and succeed in your profession. In the era of the knowledge worker, that means regular intellectual and professional updating to meet the demands of our modern technological culture. Any good leader will have an office full of those tools.

8. *Balance and Time Out*

A good leader periodically takes time away from the stresses of the job to look at his life and circumstances from a distance. Getting out of the office for business travel is one way to step back from the regular routine, but it is not really what I am referring to here. What I mean is that you must *retreat* periodically in a literal and spiritual sense from the very intense mission that is your daily fare, in order to be refreshed in soul for the mission.

The greatest leaders are always very full and vibrant people who do not neglect the needs of their souls. Pope John Paul II was a poet, a worker, a philosopher, a voracious reader in many languages, an artist, a writer, a linguist, a missionary, a churchman, an athlete, an extrovert and an introvert all at the same time. He built a swimming pool at the Vatican for exercise[6] (because a pope can't just go jogging in the park) and took retreats for the care of his soul. Yet, these times out did not diminish his productivity in his mission, which was nothing short of prodigious. We can also marvel at Pope John Paul's successor, Pope Benedict XVI, who astonished the world when everyone learned that he was a trained concert pianist.

In any area of professional life nowadays we can find extremely dedicated professional men and women who also have strong family lives and many non-work-related interests. One habit they all have in common is their insistence on taking time out from work periodically and on maintaining a balance in all areas important to them.

The interplay between action and rest is written into nature itself. Music has notes as well as silences between the notes; traffic signals have both green and red lights to keep traffic flowing; and schools have summer and winter breaks. Our Lord Jesus called Himself "Lord of the Sabbath" and urged His disciples to "come by yourselves to an out of the way place and

---

[6]   When he was criticized for spending money on a luxury item like a swimming pool, the Pope quipped that it was a lot less expensive than another conclave (i.e., the meeting of cardinals that elects a new pope)!

rest for a while" (Mark 6:31). That was two thousand years ago and I'm well assured that the Master hasn't changed His policy.

Ask yourself a few balancing questions from time to time: am I pursuing personal virtue or just greater efficiency in my profession? Have I blocked out time on my calendar for family, personal development and spiritual renewal? Do I take regular vacations? Do I read only work-related items or do I expand my intellectual universe to gain a wider perspective for my life and work?

Admittedly, it's hard to maintain balance in life. Yet, both mission effectiveness and the needs of the spirit require periodic withdrawal from the workaday world to do the essential spadework of the soul.

Conclusion

What I have tried to lay out in this chapter, and ultimately in this book, are a few basic expectations for leadership performance in the non-profit world. The principles described in these pages are not always self-evident, but they are no-nonsense understandings of how non-profits work.

Hopefully they offer some guiding standards to the tough business of leading people to better lives in this world and in the next. Competent leadership everywhere brings grace and healing to many. We generally take it for granted when it is functioning properly, but as the *Titanic* example at the beginning shows, catastrophes can be born from its absence.

It is my prayer that you will be that competent leader envisioned in the pages of this book, and in striving to live up to them, find much joy in serving your neediest brothers and sisters!

Conclusion

Potestas and Auctoritas

*Don't be Rambo. Instead, be as subtle as you
can – until you can't. And then* **lead.**

~*Jocko Willink*

S peaking of subtle, a great way to showcase an education
is to start throwing around Latin terms, so here goes:
Potestas and *Auctoritas*. You may never have heard these
words, but they have everything to do with leadership and also
are a good way to tie together all we have discussed in this book.

To boil them down to their clearest definitions, potestas
means "power" and auctoritas means "authority" (that one
was pretty easy to translate). Potestas was used by the Romans
to describe the *political, legal power* of the Roman Emperors
and their deputies, or the power implicit in military rank. It
is coercive power, by its very nature. auctoritas, on the other
hand, was used to describe the *influence* that derives from
striking personal characteristics like robust intelligence, virtue,
charisma, dynamism, vitality, spiritual giftedness, etc. It has no
sense of coercion attached to it but of attraction and persuasion.[1]

---

[1] These Latin terms are roughly equivalent to the Koine Greek terms
εξουσία (exousia: *power*) and δύναμης (dunamis: *authority*) of the
Greek New Testament.

For our purposes, these terms are useful in describing two types of human power, two qualities of a person's influence, both of which have their place and proper roles in leadership.

The Role of Potestas

If someone hires you for an executive position (in business, government, no-profit, education, etc.), you automatically receive some measure of potestas over the institution you lead. A CEO, as noted in the last chapter, inherits a full measure of legal power to run his organization on the day he assumes office: he can hire and fire; he can sign checks and freely use the assets of the company for business purposes; he controls the day-to-day operations and the employment fortunes of his associates, etc. Potestas goes with the territory of holding an office, as do the burdens of responsibility. A leader is judged to be competent if he lives up to these responsibilities, or at least if he doesn't drive the organization into the ground, legally or financially.

On the plus side, people with legal/coercive power can create change quickly in their environments: when an organization is in distress; if certain operations or programs need immediate overhaul; when incompetent managers have to be removed from entrenched positions; to meet powerful external threats, etc. Law enforcement, security guards, military forces, and courts all use coercive power to protect human society from its worst members. We should be glad when responsible people in authority use this type of power correctly – for service and protection.

A leader who wears his potestas on his sleeve, though, can be one of the worst people to work for, as witnessed by the countless employees who have had to endure overbearing personalities, arbitrary decision-making, manipulation, bullying, yelling, and the like from bad bosses.

Whenever you are put in charge of others, you have potestas, even if you are just the church choirmaster or the head of the maintenance crew. An insecure, self-important person with a bit of power can be the bane of our existence if he runs an organization that provides services we need, like the local driver's license bureau or the controlling condo association. Didn't Jesus Himself note such a tendency when He told his disciples not to be like the pagans who "lord it over others" (Matthew 20:25)?

There are many more modest forms of potestas too. Parents have authority/power to get children to do things and to punish them if they misbehave. Supervisors watch over us in most areas of life: schools and sports, jobs of all types, anything with an office, rank, boss or board. All exercise potestas.

The Role of Auctoritas

This is where auctoritas becomes relevant. Defined as persuasion or *influence*, auctoritas doesn't need an official commission of any type. It operates in any environment and has a very human face. I call it *the soul of leadership*. As I've taken pains to emphasize in this book, leadership is all about people, and human beings are more readily *influenced into doing something than coerced into it. They want to be inspired* to action, not told what to do. They can also be discouraged or scandalized by negative or failed influencers.

By its very nature, auctoritas radiates from a person as an *aura* or deep sense of confidence that appeals to the minds and hearts of others. It doesn't force behavior; it motivates people to take action and inspires them to make their own decisions. This is what makes influencers so powerful.

Advertisements claiming that "9 out of 10 doctors recommend" such-and-such a product; celebrity endorsements for a cause or product; top performers promoting something in their area of expertise: these are what we call *arguments from authority.* They marshal the aura, feeling, excitement, confidence, expertise or inspiration of influential people or groups to get you to buy what someone is selling, literally or metaphorically. It's entirely natural for people to use influence this way. Virtually everyone exercises a degree of influence over others, whether that is giving professional advice to a client, exhorting one of your children to do better in school or selling Girl Scout cookies door to door. It's all influence.

That last example reminds me of one of my friends in Scouting when I was a teenager. He was a chubby, freckle-faced kid with dimples, a perennially bad haircut and a winning smile. His personality was effervescent to the point of annoying because he never stopped talking or dreaming up wild projects, which he dragged me into, whether I liked it or not. Nevertheless, when it came time to sell tickets to the Boy Scout jamboree or chocolate bars for a troop fundraiser, my friend *shattered* all sales records every year. People just loved him and opened their wallets to buy whatever he was selling. My friend had some serious auctoritas (and is probably a very rich man today.)

On the other hand, auctoritas can also be abused: for evil or immoral purposes; for manipulation and deception; to take advantage of the ignorant or vulnerable. History has its share of cults and sects, charlatans and shysters to paint the downside of *auctoritas in living color.*

Finding the Right Balance

Some people can't be coerced but *everyone* can be influenced. A leader who is in a position to exercise potestas must do so with the moderating power of auctoritas or his leadership will lack strength and end up as a destructive force. At the same time, someone who lacks potestas may still be an effective leader over his own area of influence if he has strong auctoritas. Like my annoying friend.

Which type of leadership authority is more essential? Neither. Both are equally important for healthy human communities and organizations. Which leadership power is more effective in creating change? potestas in the short-term, auctoritas in the long-run. However, when a person integrates both qualities of power into his leadership, he is someone who can bring dramatic, transformative change to his sphere of influence.

The key leadership challenge, therefore, is to learn to integrate the two types of power into one's personal leadership style. Both powers must be held in a balance *within the leader* himself, which means that his own inner transformation – through self-awareness and mature understanding of how these powers operate – is a prerequisite to changing anyone or anything outside of him.

Let's conclude our book with the example of one effective leader who integrated these powers into an amazing life and mission that changed history.

The Leadership Competence of Joan of Arc

One of the most extraordinary leaders of all time was Joan of Arc, the 15th Century maiden who took up arms to liberate her country (France) from the occupation of a foreign power (England) and to put an end to the Hundred Years' War.

She was *only eighteen years old* when she did that. Imagine.

Auctoritas in Action

Joan of Arc had no official status for most of her short life but was full of the radiating aura of a personal and almost mystical auctoritas. She was a farm girl from a backwater region of France that was fervently loyal to the French monarch while deeply resenting their English occupiers. At age fourteen, she began to experience spiritual visions of St. Michael the Archangel, who told her that she was the one chosen by God to free her country from the grip of the English.

Over a three year period, St. Michael's messages took on the character of a specific mission for Joan: she was to go to the crown prince of France (referred to as the *dauphin*) and urge him to appoint her as head of the army. Then, she was to lift the English siege of the city of Orléans in north-central France to prevent the enemy from taking control of the whole country. After that, Joan was to bring the *dauphin*, Charles, to Rheims Cathedral to be crowned the rightful king of France. That was all.

Nothing difficult about that assignment, right?

The full story is extremely complex, and we cannot enter into more than a few details here. I encourage the reader to do his own research into Joan's fascinating story. I highly recommend starting with Mark Twain's novel, *Personal Reflections of Joan of Arc*, which is brilliant.[2]

It is enough for our purposes to say that, while still in her late teens, Joan set out on her mission to urge the political and military leaders of her day to give her command of the army so that she could drive the English out of France. This was something even the greatest military leaders of the age had been unable to do for nearly a century!

Whenever I think of Joan's fearlessness in this mission, I often wonder: What persuasive power must it have taken to convince the politicians and military men of her day to give command of their army to an illiterate teenage girl seeing visions? It's hard to imagine powerful men of *any* time or culture agreeing to an arrangement like that. The whole

---

[2]   See also this author's two books on Joan of Arc's leadership, referenced in the "Helpful Resources" at the end of this book.

venture is astonishing on its face. That Joan was successful in her quest was first and foremost a miracle of grace but also a testimony to the extraordinary personal auctoritas borne by that young woman.

Potestas in Action

Within three months of setting out on her mission of persuasion, Joan entered upon her mission of power. She received from the *dauphin* the potestas to lead the armed forces of France for the purpose of driving the occupying English forces out of their country.

Without delay, Joan launched into the campaign to lift the siege of Orléans, and everyone, from the monarch to the lowest peasant, held their collective breath to see if she would succeed. Not only did she succeed, but she scored a decisive French victory over a more powerful English force *in just one week*.

She then led her troops to an open field north of Orléans, where the two armies fought what is known to history as the lopsided Battle of Patay. In a surprise attack, the French killed as many as two thousand English soldiers in one day while losing only three sons of France in the fighting.

From there, Joan and the victorious French forces blazed a trail through 165 miles of enemy-held territory, liberated cities under English domination and successfully saw to the crowning of the *dauphin*, Charles VII, as the rightful King of France. That's as awesome an expression of sheer potestas as there ever was.

It's not hard to see that Joan of Arc wielded her military authority with lethal effectiveness, although she herself never killed anyone. She also *bristled* with personal authority in carrying out her mission, which is why so many soldiers joined the effort to liberate France under her leadership. The integration of both types of authority in the inner life of one dynamic personality profoundly changed the political relations between two nations and had an enormous effect on the future of an entire continent.

The Leadership Fusion

We cannot imitate Joan of Arc's example of heroism, and we shouldn't try. Few people in history could reproduce Joan's perfect synthesis of influence and power in the fulfillment of her mission. Yet, we can strive to achieve *our own* unique integration of virtue and authority to have an effect on our God-given missions.

To assist our efforts, let us consider a few aspects of Joan's mission, which confirm many of the lessons in this book.

- Joan of Arc believed, without question, in the goodness of her cause, and she sacrificed everything – comfort, home, family, her reputation, and ultimately, her life[3] – to accomplish it;

- Prior to her arrival on the scene, the fighting forces of France were in complete disarray and on the verge of losing both war and country to a bitter enemy; Joan rallied her disconsolate troops to heroic nobility and sacrifice in the service of a worthy cause;

- The French kingdom had been impoverished by the Black Plague and nearly eighty years of war, but Joan used the meager material assets at her disposal to carry out bold, unprecedented campaigns and achieve the most astounding victories;

---

[3]   Joan of Arc was captured by her enemies in battle, kept for a year in prison, interrogated in a three-month-long trial, and burned at the stake as a heretic on May 30th, 1431. Her enemies believed that witchcraft was the reason for her extraordinary victories, but no credible evidence could be found to convict her of that charge.

- Her leadership revivified an entire nation; prior to Joan, the French culture and traditions were merging with the dominant English culture; after Joan, the monarchy was confirmed, the unique French identity restored, and the people were once again unified.

Most importantly, Joan of Arc faithfully accomplished what she was asked to do *by God* and thus fulfilled her unique calling. In that sense, Joan of Arc was one of the most unifying spiritual figures in all of Western history, despite being a controversial figure of her day who was hated by many. Unconcerned about her own reputation, she allowed God to work *through* her. She also brought to His service a personal dynamism the likes of which has rarely been seen in the annals of warfare and culture.

Joan of Arc symbolizes, in heroic terms, the main lessons of leadership we've been examining. It's good to have heroes!

Our book began with an epic failure and ends with epic leadership success. To summarize what should be obvious by now, Joan nurtured within herself the perfect fusion of potestas and auctoritas. In contrast, Captain Smith had potestas but lacked auctoritas. Most of the real heroes of the *Titanic* lacked potestas but exercised auctoritas to a heroic degree in the service of others. The 1,500 passengers who died on the *Titanic* might never have been lost if Captain Smith had internally synthesized both dimensions of leadership. Saying this is not a judgment on the man but a leadership warning for each one of us, myself above all.

A leader can do much with potestas alone or with auctoritas alone, but it is infinitely better that a leader fuse *both* powers of leadership into a personal integration of virtue and action that always changes the world for the better. That's why we got into the incredible enterprise of non-profit work in the first place, isn't it?

Go, be Joan.

Books

David Allen, *Getting Things Done: The Art of Stress-Free Productivity*, New York: Penguin Books, 2003.

Wes Beavis, *Fuel: The Energy You Need to Succeed*, Irvine, California: Powerborn, 2009.

_____. *Fuel 2: Keeping You and Your Team Fired Up*, Irvine, California: Powerborn, 2010.

Jack Canfield, *The Success Principles: How to Get from Where You Are to Where You Want to Be*, New York: Harper, 2005.

Tom Coughlin, *Earn the Right to Win: How Success in Any Field Starts with Superior Preparation*, NY: Portfolio/Penguin, 2013.

Stephen R. Covey, *Principle-Centered Leadership*, New York: Free Press, 1991.

_____. *The Seven Habits of Highly Effective People: Powerful Lessons in Personal Change*, New York: Simon & Schuster, 1988.

Dale Carnegie Training, *Leadership Mastery: How to Challenge Yourself and Others to Greatness*, New York: Fireside, 2001.

Peter Darcy, *Joan of Arc: Leader of Men*, to be released in 2021.

_____. *The Seven Leadership Virtues of Joan of Arc*, Life-Changing Classics Series, XXXII, Boiling Springs, Pennsylvania: Tremendous Leadership, 2020.

Peter F. Drucker, *The Effective Executive*, New York: Harper and Row, 1967.

_____. *Managing Oneself and What Makes An Effective Executive*, Boston, MA: Harvard Business Review Press, 2017.

_____. *Managing the Non-Profit Organization: Principles and Practices*, New York: Harper Business, 1992.

Angela Duckworth, *Grit: The Power of Passion and Perseverance*, New York: Scribner, 2018.

Charles Duhigg, *The Power of Habit: Why We Do What We Do in Life and Business*, New York: Random House, 2012.

Hans Finzel, *The Top Ten Mistakes Leaders Make*, Colorado Springs: Cook Communications Ministries, 1994.

Tracey C. Jones, *True Blue Leadership*, Mechanicsburg, PA: Tremendous Life Books, 2011.

David H. Freedman & Charles C. Krulak, *Corps Business: The 30 Management Principles of the US Marines*, New York: HarperBusiness, 2000.

Alexandre Havard, *Virtuous Leadership: An Agenda for Personal Excellence*, Chicago: Scepter Publishers, Inc., 2007.

Gary Keller and Jay Papasan, *The ONE Thing: The Surprisingly Simple Truth Behind Extraordinary Results*, Austin: Bard Press, 2012.

Thomas à Kempis, *The Imitation of Christ*, Milwaukee: The Bruce Publishing Company, 1962.

Brad Lomenick and Mark Burnett, *H3 Leadership: Be Humble. Stay Hungry. Always Hustle*, Nashville: Nelson Books, 2016.

Chris Lowney, *Heroic Leadership: Best Practices from a 450-Year-Old Company That Changed the World*, Loyola Press: Chicago, IL, 2005.

Harvey Mackay, *Swim with the Sharks Without Being Eaten Alive: Outsell, Outmanage, Outmotivate and Outnegotiate Your Competition*, New York: Fawcett Columbine Books, 1988.

Basil Maturin, *Christian Self-Mastery: How to Govern Your Thoughts, Discipline Your Will, and Achieve Balance in Your Spiritual Life*, Manchester, NH: Sophia Institute Press, 2001.

Kelly McGonigal, *The Willpower Instinct: How Self-Control Works, Why It Matters, and What You Can Do To Get More of It*, New York: Penguin, 2013.

Tom Peters, *Leadership: Inspire, Liberate, Achieve*, New York: DK Publishing, Inc., 2005.

Nido R. Qubein, *Position Yourself for Success: 12 Proven Strategies for Uncommon Achievement*, Audio CD, Audiobook, CD, Unabridged Edition, Gildan Media, LLC, 2011.

Al Ries & Jack Trout, *The 22 Immutable Laws of Marketing*, New York: Harper, 1994.

Mark Sanborn, *You Don't Need a Title to Be a Leader: How Anyone, Anywhere, Can Make a Positive Difference*, Colorado Springs: Waterbrook Press, 2006.

Simon Sinek, *Leaders Eat Last: Why Some Teams Pull Together and Others Don't*, NY: Penguin Random House, 2014.

Michael Bungay Stanier, *The Coaching Habit: Say Less, Ask More & Change the Way You Lead Forever*, Toronto: Box of Crayons Press, 2016.

Mark Twain, *Personal Reflections of Joan of Arc,* NY: Harper & Brothers, 1896.

Jocko Willink, *Leadership, Strategy and Tactics*, NY: St. Martin's Publishing Group, 2019.

Web-Based Nonprofit Resources

Center for Nonprofit Management
(www.nonprofitanswerguide.org)

The Fundraising Authority
(www.thefundraisingauthority.com)
National Council of Nonprofits
(www.councilofnonprofits.org)
Nonprofit HR
(www.nonprofithr.com)
Nonprofit PR
(www.nonprofitPR.org)
Nonprofit Risk Management Center
(www.nonprofitrisk.org)

About the Author

Peter Darcy is an award-winning writer and editor who spent thirty years in the non-profit sector and various business enterprises. He has travelled the world attempting to do his part to bring the Kingdom of Christ to others. He recently published *The Seven Leadership Virtues of Joan of Arc* (Tremendous Leadership, 2020) and has authored or ghostwritten seven other books. Look for his book, *Joan of Arc: Leader of Men,* to come out in 2021. He is a member of the Florida Writers' Association.

9 781733 265423